WHAT I OWE
TO MY FATHER

WHAT I OWE
TO MY FATHER

by

JANE ADDAMS
ROGER W. BABSON
ALICE STONE BLACKWELL
SAMUEL A. ELIOT
EDWARD A. FILENE
HARRY EMERSON FOSDICK
JOHN HAYNES HOLMES
NICHOLAS VACHEL LINDSAY
PAUL DWIGHT MOODY
WILLIAM PICKENS
THEODORE ROOSEVELT, Jr.
OSWALD GARRISON VILLARD
STEPHEN S. WISE
MARY E. WOOLLEY

Edited by SYDNEY STRONG

with an Introduction by JAMES E. WEST

Essay Index Reprint Series

BOOKS FOR LIBRARIES PRESS
FREEPORT, NEW YORK

First Published 1931
Reprinted 1972

Library of Congress Cataloging in Publication Data

Strong, Sydney Dix, 1860-1938, ed.
    What I owe to my father.

    (Essay index reprint series)
    SUMMARY: Fourteen American men and women pay
tribute to their fathers as an important influence
in their lives.
    Reprint of the 1931 ed.
    1. U. S.--Biography--Juvenile literature.
2. Fathers--Biography--Juvenile literature.
[1. Fathers. 2. U. S.--Biography] I. Addams, Jane,
1860-1935. II. Title.
CT215.S7 1972   920.073 [920]   69-17590
ISBN 0-8369-2672-2

PRINTED IN THE UNITED STATES OF AMERICA
BY
NEW WORLD BOOK MANUFACTURING CO., INC.
HALLANDALE, FLORIDA 33009

TO AMERICAN FATHERS WHO FOR EIGHT
GENERATIONS HAVE BEEN PIONEERS IN
THE MAKING OF THE NEW WORLD,
HANDING ON THE TORCH OF FREEDOM,
PLANTING THE INSTITUTIONS OF EDU-
CATION AND RELIGION, THE EDITOR
DEDICATES THIS BOOK IN PROFOUND
APPRECIATION.

CONTENTS

CONTENTS

THE EDITOR OPENS THE BOOK

Each page in this little book carries its own credentials, tells its own story.

One story is as different from another as one father is different from another. Each story is a portrait in a gallery. As with artists, each writer while drawing his father's picture has drawn his own picture too.

None of the contributors knew what the others were writing, yet a curious spiritual unity runs throughout the book, making it almost one continuous story.

Several important phases of American life are illuminated—such as Woman's Suffrage, Slavery, and the opening of the West—and in a sense these narratives become Lights on American history. Lincoln appears twice.

The contributions are arranged in the alphabetical order of the names of the contributors. This purely mechanical plan creates a happy incident in that the book begins and ends with a woman—an Addams and a Woolley.

All the narratives, except two, were written especially for this book. There has been no attempt to harmonize them as to style; each one is presented as it came from the writer.

S. S.

New York,
February 2, 1931.

A MESSAGE TO FATHERS

It is my conviction, based on my experience, that never before has there been a finer generation of young people than that growing up in America today. They are handicapped, however, by the loose attitude of their elders towards the responsibilities of citizenship. America is today, as always, the land of opportunity, but not opportunity without obligation. American citizenship as conceived by the founders of our country makes necessary constant vigilance on the part of all of us, especially in view of present-day conditions, to maintain that attitude of mind that regards citizenship as a responsibility and not a privilege alone.

America cannot improve by increasing laws or improving laws, or even by improving judicial procedure. The great hope lies in impressing upon young people at an early age a sense of personal responsibility. This is a matter of personal concern to every parent, for there is no agency so far reaching in the development of standards as the home. This is a challenge to the best that is within us. Let us rededicate ourselves to it, to the end that we may exert greater influence in the lives of the young people of today, who as citizens tomorrow will be leaders in the affairs of our nation and of the world.—JAMES E. WEST, *Chief Scout Executive, Boy Scouts of America.*

SPEAKING FOR THE BOYS OF THE WORLD

The Editor's cable of January 21, 1931, to Tracy Strong, Editor of *The World's Youth*, and member of the World's Committee of the Young Men's Christian Association, Geneva, Switzerland:

> PLEASE CABLE FIFTY WORDS KIND OF FATHERS
> BOYS OF WORLD DEMANDING
>
> SYDNEY STRONG

Answer of January 23, 1931:

UNIVERSAL REQUIREMENTS FOOD SHELTER COUNSEL.

NATIONAL RACIAL DEMANDS VARY:
JAPAN AUTHORITY COURTESY;
INDIA PASSION FOR SPIRITUAL IDEALS;
CHINA TO BE WORTHY OF WORSHIP;
BRITISH FAIR PLAY;
RUSSIAN WILLINGNESS TO TRY UNTRIED THINGS;
SLAVIC PATIENT IDEALISM;
LATIN CULTURE;
AFRICAN HUMOR PATHOS;
NORTH AMERICAN DEMOCRATIC COMRADESHIP.
THESE COMBINED CHARACTERISTICS APPROACH PERFECTION.

WORLD NEEDS FATHERS WHO LOVE WORLD'S BOYHOOD AS OWN.
CHRIST REVEALS FATHERHOOD SUFFERING LOVE.

TRACY STRONG

To

JOHN H. ADDAMS

by

JANE ADDAMS

Hull House, Chicago

I had a consuming ambition to possess a miller's thumb. . . . I believe I have never since wanted anything more desperately than I wanted my right thumb to be flattened, as my father's had become during his earlier years of a miller's life. . . .

*   *   *   *

Once again I heard his testimony in favor of "mental integrity above everything else." . . .

JANE ADDAMS

ALL of the impressions of my childhood are directly connected with my father, although of course I recall many experiences apart from him. I was one of the younger members of a large family and an eager participant in the village life, but because my father was so distinctly the dominant influence and because it is quite impossible to set forth all of one's early impressions, it has seemed simpler to string these first memories on that single cord. Moreover, it was this cord which not only held fast my supreme affection, but also first drew me into the moral concerns of life, and later afforded a clew there to which I somewhat wistfully clung in the intricacy of its mazes.

It must have been at a very early period that I recall "horrid nights" when I tossed about in my bed because I had told a lie. I was held in the grip of a miserable dread of death, a double fear, first, that I myself should die in my sins and go straight to that fiery Hell which was never mentioned at home, but which I had heard all about from other children, and, second, that my father—representing the entire adult world which I had basely deceived—should himself die before I had time to tell him.

My only method of obtaining relief was to go downstairs to my father's room and make full confession. The high resolve to do this would push me out of bed and carry me down the stairs without a touch of fear. But at the foot of the stairs I would be faced by the awful necessity of passing the front door—which my father, because of his Quaker tendencies, did not lock —and of crossing the wide and black expanse of the living room in order to reach his door. I would invariably cling to the newel post while I contemplated the perils of the situation, complicated by the fact that the literal first step meant putting my bare foot upon a piece of oilcloth in front of the door, only a few inches wide, but lying straight in my path. I would finally reach my father's bedside perfectly breathless and, having panted out the history of my sin, invariably would receive the same assurance that if he "had a little girl who told lies" he was very glad that she "felt too bad to go to sleep afterwards."

No absolution was asked for nor received, but apparently the sense that the knowledge of my wicked ness was shared, or an obscure understanding of the affection which underlay the grave statement, was sufficient, for I always went back to bed as bold as a lion, and slept, if not the sleep of the righteous, at least that of the comforted.

I recall an incident which must have occurred before I was seven years old, for the mill in which my father transacted his business that day was closed in 1867. The mill stood in the neighboring town adjacent to its poorest quarter. Before then I had always seen the little city of ten thousand people with the admiring eyes of a country child, and it had never occurred to me that all its streets were not as bewilderingly attractive as the one which contained the glittering toyshop and the confectioner. On that day I had my first sight of the poverty which implies squalor, and felt the curious distinction between the ruddy poverty of the country and that which even a small city presents in its shabbiest streets. I remember launching at my father the pertinent inquiry why people lived in such horrid little houses so close together and that after receiving his explanation I declared with much firmness when I grew up I should, of course, have a large house, but it would not be built among the other large houses, but right in the midst of horrid little houses like these.

My great veneration and pride in my father manifested itself in curious ways. On several Sundays, doubtless occurring in two or three different years, the Union Sunday School of the village was visited by strangers, some of those "strange people" who live outside a child's realm, yet constantly thrill it by their close approach. My father taught the large Bible class in the left-hand corner of the church next to the pulpit, and to my eyes at least, was a most imposing figure in his Sunday frock coat, his fine head rising high above all the others. I imagined that the strangers were filled with admiration for this dignified person, and I prayed with all my heart that the ugly, pigeon-toed little girl, whose crooked back obliged her to walk with her head held very much upon one side, would never be pointed out to these visitors as the daughter of this fine man. In order to lessen the possibility of a connection being made, on these Sundays I did not walk beside my father, although this walk was the great event of the week, but attached myself firmly to the side of my Uncle James Addams, in the hope that I should be mistaken for his child, or at least that I should not remain so conspicuously unattached that troublesome questions might identify an Ugly Duckling with her imposing parent. My uncle, who had many children of his own, must have been mildly surprised at this unwonted attention, but he would look down kindly at me and say, "So you are going to walk with me today?" "Yes, please, Uncle James," would be my meek reply. He fortunately never explored my motives, nor do I remember that my father ever did, so that in all probability my machinations have been safe from public knowledge until this hour.

It is hard to account for the manifestations of a child's adoring affection, so emotional, so irrational, so tangled with the affairs of the imagination. I simply could not endure the thought that "strange people" should know that my handsome father owned this homely little girl. But even in my chivalric desire to protect him from his fate, I was not quite easy in the sacrifice of my uncle, although I quieted my scruples with the reflection that the contrast was less marked and that, anyway, his own little girl "was not so very pretty." I do not know that I commonly dwelt much upon my personal appearance, save as it thrust itself

as an incongruity into my father's life, and in spite of
unending evidence to the contrary, there were even
black moments when I allowed myself to speculate as
to whether he might not share the feeling. Happily,
however, this specter was laid before it had time to
grow into a morbid familiar by a very trifling incident.
One day I met my father coming out of his bank on the
main street of the neighboring city which seemed to
me a veritable whirlpool of society and commerce. With
a playful touch of exaggeration, he lifted his high and
shining silk hat and made me an imposing bow. This
distinguished public recognition, this totally unneces-
sary identification among a mass of "strange people"
who couldn't possibly know unless he himself made the
sign, suddenly filled me with a sense of the absurdity
of the entire feeling. It may not even then have seemed
as absurd as it really was, but at least it seemed enough
so to collapse or to pass into the limbo of forgotten
specters.

I made still other almost equally grotesque attempts
to express this doglike affection. The house at the end
of the village in which I was born, and which was my
home until I moved to Hull House, in my earliest childhood had opposite to it—only across the road and then
across a little stretch of greensward—two mills belong-
ing to my father; one flour mill, to which the various
grains were brought by the neighboring farmers, and
one sawmill, in which the logs of the native timber
were sawed into lumber.

In addition to these fascinations was the association

of the mill with my father's activities, for doubtless at that time I centered upon him all that careful imitation which a little girl ordinarily gives to her mother's ways and habits. My mother had died when I was a baby and my father's second marriage did not occur until my eighth year.

I had a consuming ambition to possess a miller's thumb, and would sit contentedly for a long time rubbing between my thumb and fingers the ground wheat as it fell from between the millstones, before it was taken up on an endless chain of mysterious little buckets to be bolted into flour. I believe I have never since wanted anything more desperately than I wanted my right thumb to be flattened, as my father's had become, during his earlier years of a miller's life.

This sincere tribute of imitation, which affection offers to its adored object, had later, I hope, subtler manifestations, but certainly these first ones were altogether genuine. In this case, too, I doubtless contributed my share to that stream of admiration which our generation so generously poured forth for the self-made man. I was consumed by a wistful desire to apprehend the hardships of my father's earlier life in that far away time when he had been a miller's apprentice. I know that he still woke up punctually at three o'clock because for so many years he had taken his turn at the mill in the early morning, and if by chance I awoke at the same hour, as curiously enough I often did, I imagined him in the early dawn in my uncle's old mill reading through the entire village library, book after book, beginning with the lives of the signers of the Declaration of Independence. Copies of the same books, mostly bound in calfskin, were to be found in the library below, and I courageously resolved that I too would read them all and try to understand life as he did. I did in fact later begin a course of reading in the early morning hours, but I was caught by some fantastic notion of chronological order and early legendary form. Pope's translation of the "Iliad," even followed by Dryden's "Virgil," did not leave behind the residuum of wisdom for which I longed, and I finally gave them up for a thick book entitled "The History of the World" as affording a shorter and an easier path.

Although I constantly confided my sins and perplexities to my father, there are only a few occasions on which I remember having received direct advice or admonition; it may easily be true, however, that I have forgotten the latter, in the manner of many seekers after advice who enjoyably set forth their situation but do not really listen to the advice itself. I can remember an admonition on one occasion, however, when, as a little girl of eight years, arrayed in a new cloak, gorgeous beyond anything I had ever worn before, I stood before my father for his approval. I was much chagrined by his remark that it was a very pretty cloak—in fact so much prettier than any cloak the other little girls in the Sunday School had, that he would advise me to wear my old cloak which would keep me quite as warm, with the added advantage of not making the other little girls feel badly.

I complied with the request but I fear without inner consent, and I certainly was quite without the joy of self-sacrifice as I walked soberly through the village street by the side of my counselor. My mind was busy, however, with the old question eternally suggested by the inequalities of the human lot. Only as we neared the church door did I venture to ask what could be done about it, receiving the reply that it might never be righted so far as clothes went, but that people might be equal in things that mattered much more than clothes, the affairs of education and religion, for instance, which we attended to when we went to school and church, and that it was very stupid to wear the sort of clothes that made it harder to have equality even there.

It must have been a little later when I held a conversation with my father about the doctrine of foreordination, which at one time very much perplexed my childish mind. After setting the difficulty before him and complaining that I could not make it out, although my best friend "understood it perfectly," I settled down to hear his argument, having no doubt that he could make it quite clear. To my delighted surprise, for any intimation that our minds were on an equality lifted me high indeed, he said that he feared that he and I did not have the kind of mind that would ever understand foreordination very well and advised me not to give too much time to it; but he then proceeded to say other things of which the final impression left upon my mind was, that it did not matter much whether one understood foreordination or not, but that it was very important not to pretend to understand what you didn't understand and that you must always be honest with yourself inside, whatever happened. Perhaps on the whole as valuable a lesson as the shorter catechism itself contains.

My memory merges this early conversation on religious doctrine into one which took place years later when I put before my father the situation in which I found myself at boarding school when under great evangelical pressure, and once again I heard his testimony in favor of "mental integrity above everything else."

At the time we were driving through a piece of timber in which the wood choppers had been at work during the winter, and so earnestly were we talking that he suddenly drew up the horses to find that he did not know where he was. We were both entertained by the incident, I that my father had been "lost in his own timber" so that various cords of wood must have escaped his practiced eye, and he on his side that he should have become so absorbed in this maze of youthful speculation. We were in high spirits as we emerged from the tender green of the spring woods into the clear light of day, and as we came back into the main road I categorically asked him: "What are you? What do you say when people ask you?"

His eyes twinkled a little as he soberly replied:

"I am a Quaker."

"But that isn't enough to say," I urged.

"Very well," he added, "to people who insist upon details, as some one is doing now, I add that I am a Hicksite Quaker"; and not another word on the weighty subject could I induce him to utter.

I recall with great distinctness my first direct contact with death when I was fifteen years old: Polly was an old nurse who had taken care of my mother and had followed her to frontier Illinois to help rear a second generation of children. She had always lived in our house, but made annual visits to her cousins on a farm a few miles north of the village. During one of these visits, word came to us one Sunday evening that Polly was dying, and for a number of reasons I was the only person able to go to her. An hour after my arrival all of the cousin's family went downstairs to supper, and I was left alone to watch with Polly. The square, old-fashioned chamber in the lonely farmhouse was very cold and still, with nothing to be heard but the storm outside. Suddenly the great change came. I heard a feeble call of "Sarah," my mother's name, as the dying eyes were turned upon me, followed by a curious breathing and in place of the face familiar from my earliest childhood and associated with homely household cares, there lay upon the pillow strange, august features, stern and withdrawn from all the small affairs of life. That sense of solitude, of being unsheltered in a wide world of relentless and elemental forces which is at the basis of childhood's timidity and which is far from outgrown at fifteen, seized me irresistibly before I could reach the narrow stairs and summon the family from below.

As I was driven home in the winter storm, the wind through the trees seemed laden with a passing soul and the riddle of life and death pressed hard; once to be young, to grow old and to die, everything came to that, and then a mysterious journey out into the Unknown. Did she mind faring forth alone? Would the journey perhaps end in something as familiar and natural to the aged and dying as life is to the young and living? Through all the drive and indeed throughout the night these thoughts were pierced by sharp worry, a sense of faithlessness because I had forgotten the text Polly had confided to me long before as the one from which she wished her funeral sermon to be preached. My comfort as usual finally came from my father, who pointed out what was essential and what was of little avail even in such a moment as this, and while he was much too wise to grow dogmatic upon the great theme of death, I felt a new fellowship with him because we had discussed it together.

An incident which stands out clearly in my mind as an exciting suggestion of the great world of moral enterprise and serious undertakings, must have occurred earlier than this, for in 1872, when I was not yet twelve years old, I came into my father's room one morning to find him sitting beside the fire with a newspaper in his hand, looking very solemn; and upon my eager inquiry about what had happened, he told me that Joseph Mazzini was dead. I had never even heard Mazzini's name, and after being told about him I was inclined to grow argumentative, asserting that my father did not know him, that he was not an American, and that I could not understand why we should be expected to feel badly about him. It is impossible to recall the conversation with the complete breakdown of my cheap arguments, but in the end I obtained that which I have ever regarded as a valuable possession, a sense of the genuine relationship which may exist between men who share large hopes and like desires, even though they differ in nationality, language, and creed; that those things count for absolutely nothing between groups of men who are trying to abolish slavery in America or to throw off Hapsburg oppression in Italy.

At any rate, I was heartily ashamed of my meager notion of patriotism, and I came out of the room exhilarated with the consciousness that impersonal and international relations are actual facts and not mere phrases. I was filled with pride that I knew a man who held converse with great minds and who really sorrowed and rejoiced over happenings across the sea. I never recall those early conversations with my father, nor a score of others like them, but there comes into my mind a line from Mrs. Browning in which a daughter describes her relations with her father:

> "He wrapt me in his large
> Man's doublet, careless did it fit or no."

I suppose all the children who were born about the time of the Civil War have recollections quite unlike

those of the children who are living now. Although I
was but four and a half years old when Lincoln died,
I distinctly remember the day when I found on our two
white gate posts American flags companioned with
black. I tumbled down on the harsh gravel walk in my
eager rush into the house to inquire what they were
"there for." To my amazement I found my father in
tears, something that I had never seen before, having
assumed, as all children do, that grown-up people never
cried. The two flags, my father's tears and his impressive statement that the greatest man in the world
had died, constituted my initiation, my baptism, as it
were, into the thrilling and solemn interests of a world
lying quite outside the two white gate posts.

Thousands of children in the sixties and seventies,
in the simplicity which is given to the understanding of
a child, caught a notion of imperishable heroism when
they were told that brave men had lost their lives that
the slaves might be free. At any moment the conversation of our elders might turn upon these heroic events;
there were red-letter days, when a certain general came
to see my father, and again when Governor Oglesby,
whom all Illinois children called "Uncle Dick," spent a
Sunday under the pine trees in our front yard. We felt
on those days a connection with the great world so
much more heroic than the village world which surrounded us through all the other days. My father was
a member of the state senate for the sixteen years between 1854 and 1870, and even as a little child I was

dimly conscious of the grave march of public affairs in his comings and goings at the state capital.

My father always spoke of the martyred President as Mr. Lincoln, and I never heard the great name without a thrill. I remember the day—it must have been one of comparative leisure, perhaps a Sunday—when at my request my father took out of his desk a thin packet marked "Mr. Lincoln's Letters," even the shortest one of which bore unmistakable traces of that remarkable personality. These letters began, "My dear Double-D'ed Addams," and to the inquiry as to how the person thus addressed was about to vote on a certain measure then before the legislature, was added the assurance that he knew that this Addams "would vote according to his conscience," but he begged to know in what direction the same conscience "was pointing." As my father folded up the bits of paper I fairly held my breath in my desire that he should go on with the reminiscence of this wonderful man, whom he had known in his comparative obscurity, or better still, that he should be moved to tell some of the exciting incidents of the Lincoln-Douglas debates. There were at least two pictures of Lincoln that always hung in my father's room, and one in our old-fashioned upstairs parlor, of Lincoln with Little Tad. For one or all of these reasons I always tend to associate Lincoln with the tenderest thoughts of my father.

Of the many things written of my father in that sad August in 1881, when he died, the one I cared for most was written by an old political friend of his who was then editor of a great Chicago daily. He wrote that while there were doubtless many members of the Illinois legislature who during the great contracts of the war time and the demoralizing reconstruction days that followed, had never accepted a bribe, he wished to bear testimony that he personally had known but this one man who had never been offered a bribe because bad men were instinctively afraid of him.

I feel now the hot chagrin with which I recalled this statement during those early efforts of Illinois in which Hull House joined, to secure the passage of the first factory legislation. I was told by the representatives of an informal association of manufacturers that if the residents of Hull House would drop this nonsense about a sweat shop bill, of which they knew nothing, certain business men would agree to give fifty thousand dollars within two years to be used for any of the philanthropic activities of the Settlement. As the fact broke upon me that I was being offered a bribe, the shame was enormously increased by the memory of this statement. What had befallen the daughter of my father that such a thing could happen to her?

The salutary reflection that it could not have occurred unless a weakness in myself had permitted it, withheld me at least from an heroic display of indignation before the two men making the offer, and I explained as gently as I could that we had no ambition to make Hull House "the largest institution of the West Side," but that we were much concerned that our neighbors should be protected from untoward conditions of work, and—so much heroics, youth must permit itself—if to accomplish this the destruction of Hull House was necessary, that we would cheerfully sing a Te Deum on its ruins.

To

NATHANIEL BABSON

by

ROGER W. BABSON

Wellesley Hills, Massachusetts

Looking back upon the great wisdom of my father, I cannot help thinking how utterly wasteful of advice children are. . . .

* * * *

To quote my father: "What is needed is not the crushing of natural instincts, but the harnessing of their energy to some great and satisfying objective."

ROGER W. BABSON

I HAVE been especially blessed by having had my father and mother until I was 55 years of age. Both passed away at the ripe age of 76 years and within a comparatively short time of one another. Therefore, my contacts with them both—especially my father—were very close. I was very fortunate in having them live so long, because each so well supplemented the other. My mother was very active and emotional, while my father was very quiet and conservative. Mother was the one to whom Gloucester people appealed when they wanted quick action;—that is, "something done." Father was the one to whom they appealed when they wanted *mature judgment*. His opinions on business and financial matters were constantly sought and invariably right. My parents were perfect mates from the view of the psychologists, who say that the best marriages are between those having "like tastes, but opposite dispositions."

Looking back upon the great wisdom of my father, I cannot help thinking how utterly wasteful of advice children are. We not only seldom asked for it; but usually forgot it when it was given to us. Yet any parent or friend is willing to give, without price, *the very valuable results of his long years of life and struggle.* We usually are either too busy or too proud to ask for such counsel. Surely this is a great mistake. Much more often

21

I could have gone to my father for some good advice. It would have made him proud and happy if I had done so. The talks would have been worth much to me. In fact, I always had planned to do it, although as it is I owe my parents for all the training I have. I loved my father dearly and he was a very wonderful man. But today it is too late. His spirit has fled. No wealth nor power can call it back. *I am too late.* However, I am very thankful for the advice I did seek and only write these words hoping they may cause readers who have parents living to grasp the golden opportunity which they now have.

What a mistake we make in giving so much time to business and so little to our parents and families. Surely there is no logic in the excuse that "we are working for them." Our families do not want us to leave them with a bigger business. *They want more of us.* Besides, the profession or industry in which we are engaged can be developed any time; but we have only a few years here at most. Let us use them sensibly and quit chasing one another like squirrels in a cage. Besides, there are thousands of men who are anxious and able to do what we are doing in business; while no other person in the whole wide world can take our place in the old home. Therefore, let those of you readers who have parents give them more time. Call upon them more often. Talk things over with them more than you do. Never let a week go by without writing to them. Someone else can take your place in almost every other job, excepting in the job of being a faithful son or daughter.

One word to fathers: Don't wait too long before taking your children into your confidence. Don't figure that you'll know when you are in your last sickness, thinking then will be time enough to make plans. Don't hesitate to talk freely now about what you would like done after you are gone. *This very night take your children into your library and open to them your heart. Tell them of your plans and hopes; how you would like the business carried on; whom you would promote to positions of responsibility, and what you would like your children to do. In every talk which I give to the Babson Institute students I appeal to them to go to their fathers for advice on every opportunity.* Not only are children losing golden opportunities by not talking more with their parents, but parents are missing even greater opportunities by not talking more with their children.

My father was a very *sanely* religious man. He was active in the Trinity Congregational Church of Gloucester, Mass., having been a member of the Prudential Committee for about fifty years and a Deacon for twenty-five years. For a long period he had a large Sunday School class of men and was a leader in all movements for raising funds in connection with building and maintenance of the church. I, however, especially remember him for his rational religious faith. It appealed to me as a trained engineer and statistician.

My father honestly believed that everything worked together for the best for those who do right. Romans 8:28 was his favorite verse. He believed in both the purpose of pain and the reality of conscience. When he felt unwell—as he often did—it was a message from God that he was doing something which he should not or was not doing something which he should do. In the same way, he listened very seriously to his conscience, —or to "God speaking from within." As the sense of pain warned him of physical errors, so the sense of conscience warned him of spiritual errors. He believed that a spiritual power was constantly guiding him and —so long as he did his best—the result was always for the best.

When asking famous physicians what one fact of their studies is most significant, the usual common reply is: *The way in which the chemistry of the body is constantly working to make for growth and perfect health.* By this statement these physicians mean that all we need for health is to "let nature alone" and not abuse it. If we behave ourselves, we can absolutely trust chemistry to make a strong and beautiful body. Moreover, the best physicians are continually giving less and less medicine, but are prescribing merely rest, good food, and sunshine. Studies show that if the sick one will rest and take proper nourishment, chemistry will of itself make the cure. Chemistry seems, consciously or unconsciously, to seek a goal of perfect health if we will give it a chance. This was the basis of my father's philosophy as to physical health and on this philosophy I was raised and trained.

As *chemistry* controls the physical side of our lives and determines our health, size and appearance, so my father believed that *spirituality* controls our intellectual side and determines our instincts, emotions and thoughts. As the latter are such very important factors in the happiness of us all, the spiritual forces are even more vital to our everyday lives than the physical forces. During my father's days, men had been concentrating on the physical sciences. There had been such an evident opportunity to make progress in physics, chemistry, biology and otherwise, that the laboratory workers had not got around to studying the spiritual. My father believed, however, that as people learn that all the chemistry, electricity and wealth in the world cannot make people happy, these master minds will turn their laboratories over to a study of the spiritual and intangible. There are already evidences of this in connection with the new movement in physics. The leading physicists of today are the humblest of men in their awe of unseen power.

Experience—which is now the basis of the latest scientific work—shows that my father was right in that the *Spirit* of the body is constantly working to make for growth and perfect happiness. By this is meant that all we need in order to be happy is to do right and trust God.[1] If we have the right desires, my father believed we can absolutely trust the Spirit to make a useful and happy personality. This is the meaning of the words: *"And we know that all things work together for good to them who love God, to them who are called*

---

[1] My father would say: "God is the name by which this spiritual power is commonly known." St. John 4: 24.

according to his purpose." Those who have the right
desires have no cause to worry. We can trust the Spirit
of the body so to direct our judgments, thoughts and
actions as to give success and happiness, just as truly
as we can depend upon the chemicals of the body to
give us health and beauty. Spirituality, consciously or
unconsciously, seeks a goal of happiness if we will give
it a chance. Just as the physicians are now trusting
"nature" to cure their patients, so we can trust the Holy
Spirit to give us judgment and self-control.

My father always felt that a greater interest should
be aroused in collecting and studying data on religious
experiences. He felt that the church and especially the
theological schools are weak in their "cases." He believed that the same "case method" used in teaching
the sciences should be used in teaching theology. He
felt that if the theological seminaries would only take
the trouble to do this necessary laboratory work, the
results would be astounding. My father was a great believer in the power of prayer and he always had family
prayers every Sunday night up to the time of his death.
In this connection, I wish to pass along an illustration
of my present pastor, Rev. Carl M. Gates, which so
well illustrates my father's ideas.

Many solar motors have been patented. One—to
which I will refer—was patented by a professor in
Clark University. A mirror catches the sun's rays and
focusses them on a mass of water into which mercury at
high pressure has been sprayed. The intense heat
changes the water and mercury into vapor at high pres-

sure and this vapor is carried to turbine engines. According to the inventor, a mirror 100 feet in diameter could generate 650 horsepower energy. This is typical of many attempts which are being made in any number of laboratories. If only the power which is going to waste can be utilized, it will mean both the possibility of new achievements and the saving of men's energies for more important uses. Oh—how often have I heard my father talk along these lines!

We are alive to the importance of harnessing the material forces of the universe, but we are slow to realize the still greater need of using to the utmost the mental and spiritual energies which are available. Think of the power hidden away in the emotions which is now going to waste! Our feelings run away with us, leaping from one object to another without the least semblance of control, like the water in a cataract, instead of being guided into channels where their marvellous possibilities can be utilized to make the whole world richer and better. Many of the ills from which society is suffering today are due to undisciplined feelings. People do what the mood of the moment impels them to without any regard to the ultimate effects. To quote my father: "What is needed is not the crushing of natural instincts, but the harnessing of their energy to some great and satisfying objective."

Scientists estimate that there is energy enough in less than 50 acres of sunshine to run all the machinery of the world if it could be concentrated. But the sun might blaze out upon the earth forever without setting anything on fire. Focus the same rays by a burning glass and they would melt solid granite or change a diamond into vapor. So it is the concentration along spiritual lines that gives a man strength and effectiveness. A great many folks today have plenty of speed, but no definite spiritual goal. So, rushing madly from one thing to another, the lasting accomplishments of the lives of a great many business men are pathetically few. The latent power of the spiritual life, including prayer, love and right living, are even far greater than any latent material power. My father both believed in such latent spiritual power and was an example of its force.

My father was brought up in business and devoted his life thereto. He went to work as clerk in a dry goods store when a young boy and gradually climbed up until he had the leading dry goods store in Gloucester. Then he retired and devoted himself to banking and the care of his investments. But he kept in very close touch with all scientific developments. He was especially interested in the studies of Millikan, Pupin and Eddington. I cannot do better than close this article by quoting from Sir Arthur Eddington as illustrative of my father's dreams. Although the new movement in physics came only during his later years, he was keenly aware of the far-reaching possibilities of such physical studies.

"Materialism and determinism, those household gods of nineteenth-century science which believed that the world could be explained in mechanical concepts as a well-run machine, must be discarded by modern science.

Materialism must give way for a spiritual conception of the universe and man's place in it, with religion supplementing that part of the picture which science now must acknowledge itself unable to paint.

"There have been striking changes of scientific views, and one of these is in regard to determinism, the view that the future is pre-destined and that time merely turns over the leaves of a story that is already written. Until recently, this was almost universally accepted as the teaching of science, at least in regard to the material universe. It is the distinctive principle of the mechanistic outlook which some years ago superseded the crude materialistic answer. But today physical theory is not mechanistic. The most scientific physical teaching of today is built on a foundation which knows nothing of this supposed determination. So far as we have yet gone in our probing of the material universe we cannot find a particle of evidence in favor of determination.

"There is no longer, I think, any need to doubt our intuition of free will. Our minds are not merely registering a pre-determined sequence of thoughts and decisions. Our faculties and purposes are genuine, and ours is the responsibility for what ensues from them. We must admit that, for we are scarcely likely to accept a theory which would make the human spirit more mechanistic than the physical universe. In fact, any of the young theoretical physicists of today will tell you that the basis of all the phenomena coming within their province is a scheme of symbols connected by mathematical equations. This is what the physical universe boils down to when probed by the methods which a physicist can apply,—a skeleton scheme of symbols.

"It seems to me that the time has come when we scientists can no longer point to the result and say:

This is you. We will say rather: This is how I symbolize you in my description and explanation of your properties which I can observe. If you claim any deeper insight into your own nature, any knowledge of what it is that these symbols symbolize, you can rest assured that I have no other interpretation of the symbols to propose.

"I would say that when from the human heart the cry goes up—'What is it all about?' It is no true answer to look only at that part of experience which comes to us through certain sensory organs and reply: 'It is about the atoms and chaos, it is about a universe of fiery globes moving on to impending doom; it is about non-computated algebra'; but rather it is about a *Spirit* in which truth has its shrine, with potentialities of self-fulfilment in its response to right and truth. It is the essence of religion that presents this side of experience as a matter of everyday life. To live in it we have to grasp it in the form of familiar recognition and not as a series of abstract statements. Its counterpart in our outward life is the familiar world and not the symbolic scientific universe.

"It means a great deal to me to conceive of God as him through whom come power and guidance. But just because it means so much I have no use for it if it is only fiction which will not stand close examination. Can we not give some assurance that there is such a God in reality and that belief in him is not merely a sop to my limited imagination? I believe that we can. I am convinced that if in physics we pursue to the bitter end our attempt to reach purely objective reality, we would simply undo the work of creation and present the world as we might conceive it to have been before the spirit moved on the face of the waters. The spiritual element in our experience is the creative element, and if we remove it, on the ground that it always creates an illusion we must reach what was in the beginning."

The above are the words of one of the world's leading scientists; but they represent the religion of my father and the basis of my personal faith. This is the faith upon which the Babson Institute was founded. As my father's picture looks down upon the students in the main library, it seems to say:

"Keep your head in the clouds; but keep your feet on the ground. Combine a *sane faith* with *hard work*. Lead a well-balanced life with a fair amount of *work* and *play—love* and *faith*. Give heed to your health; attend to your business; save your pennies and say your prayers; but do not become 'hipped' upon any one of these things. No one of these four—health, enterprise, thrift or prayers—will bring happiness. Happiness comes only as a proper mixture of them all and others besides. Also remember that real joy comes in the *striving*, rather than in the *arriving*."

To

HENRY B. BLACKWELL

by

ALICE STONE BLACKWELL

Boston

A tribute to Henry B. Blackwell by Theodore Winthrop in "Edwin Brothertoft."

"It is a mighty influence when the portrait of a noble forefather puts its eye on one who wears his name, and says, by the language of an unchanging look: 'I was a Radical in my day; be thou the same in thine!' I turned my back upon the old tyrannies and heresies, and struck for the new liberties and beliefs; my liberty and belief are doubtless already tyranny and heresy to thine age; strike thou for the new! I worshipped the purest God of my generation—it may be that a purer God is revealed to thine; worship him with thy whole heart."

ALICE STONE BLACKWELL

MY debt to my father is twofold, as a daughter and as a woman. He was not only a kind and loving father, but a powerful champion of equal rights for women. Many prominent men in America, from Abraham Lincoln down, favored woman suffrage, and not a few did valiant work for it; but Henry B. Blackwell was the one man of high talents who really devoted his life to that cause.

I will speak first of my debt to him as a daughter. He transmitted to me a sound heredity on his own side, and he gave me a good mother. These are probably the greatest boons that any father can bestow upon a child. A young man was once asked by his friends why he did not try to marry a certain very beautiful but rather frivolous girl. He said, "Is she a person whom you would pick out to entrust with the bringing up of your children?" They had to admit that she was not. He answered, "Well, I do not choose to entrust her with the bringing up of mine." My father did not make that mistake.

He also handed down to me a fine family tradition of public spirit and public service. Born in Bristol, England, May 4, 1825, he came to this country with his parents at seven years old. His father, Samuel Blackwell, was a sugar-refiner, and set up in New York the first vacuum pans ever used in America. His business

brought him in contact with slaveholders from the West
Indies and elsewhere, and he was shocked at their attitude and that of the public towards the slaves. He
joined the Anti-Slavery Society, and wrote a volume of
"Slavery Rhymes," which he published anonymously,
because slavery was then an "American institution,"
and any criticism of American institutions by a for-
eigner aroused the ire of those opposed to improvement,
just as it does today. When George Thompson came
over from England to help the abolitionists, his presence
was made a pretext for mob violence.

The Blackwell family worked for the Anti-Slavery
Fairs, and little Henry, who wrote a handsome hand,
copied out antislavery mottoes to be wrapped up with
the candies. When it was unsafe for William Lloyd
Garrison to pass the night in New York City, he passed
it at the Blackwell home on Long Island. Dr. Abram
Cox also took refuge there when the mob of New York
rose against him because he had said, in an antislavery
sermon, that Jesus did not belong to the Caucasian
race, and word went out that he had said "Jesus Christ
was a nigger."

A few years later, Mr. Blackwell moved to Cincinnati, partly with the hope of introducing the cultivation
of beet sugar, and thus indirectly striking a heavy blow
at the slave-grown cane sugar of the South; but he died
soon after his arrival. The widow and elder daughters
opened a school for girls, and supported the family till
the sons, all of whom were younger, were able to earn.
Henry helped his mother by acting as cook for the

family. All his life he was ready to lend a cheerful and energetic hand with the housework. He was given a year at Kemper College, near St. Louis. Here he distinguished himself greatly in his studies; but the family finances did not allow him to stay longer. At fourteen, he became an office boy, at $2 per week. At twenty, he was the manager of two mills. With the money earned in the milling business, he bought a small brick house at Walnut Hills, a suburb of Cincinnati. Characteristically, he placed the house in his mother's name. It was the family home for years. It was close to Lane Seminary, and Harriet Beecher Stowe and her husband were their neighbors and friends.

Henry was a young man full of life and vivacity. He had curly black hair, blue eyes, remarkably bright and sparkling, and such beautiful teeth that his friends nicknamed him Carker, after the villain with glittering teeth in "Dombey and Son." He had a kind heart and a most chivalrous disposition. He was a good writer, an eloquent speaker, and a fine singer. There is a saying, "A merry heart doeth good like medicine." Henry overflowed by nature with wit and fun. He kept everybody laughing; and, as everybody likes to laugh, he was a great social favorite. In addition, he was an active and capable man of business. He became partner in a hardware firm, and for seven years he travelled on horseback, through Indiana, Ohio, Illinois and Wisconsin, securing orders; journeying often over unfathomably muddy roads, sometimes riding many miles by compass through unbroken forest, sleeping in log cabins, and meeting the plain people of the Middle West in a way that he always said was worth more to him than a college education. He worked in malarious regions where it was popularly believed that the only way for people to escape fever and ague was to keep themselves soaked in whiskey; but he steered clear of liquor, and remained well. He also kept up his English habit of a daily cold bath, though he often passed the night in primitive pioneer shanties where there was sometimes not even a wash-basin. He carried with him a rubber sheet with a broad hem, through which a rope was passed. Laying the sheet on the floor, he would set a pail of water on it and take a sponge bath; then pick up the sheet by the corners and pour the water back into the pail. This device may still be found useful by those who travel where there are no bath-tubs, or who cannot afford a "room with bath."

He built up a large trade in the Wabash Valley. In addition, he obtained a quantity of wild lands. He wrote, long after:

"Wisconsin, wishing to use for school purposes the magnificent grant of wild lands made by the United States government, offered them in lots of forty acres each, on thirty years' credit, at $1.25 per acre; and its sixteenth section lands on ten years' credit. A friend suggested that I should go out and select a few thousand acres for him and myself. Having plenty of youthful energy, and very little money, I accepted, and in a single forenoon enlisted a number of other merchants, my friends, in an arrangement to locate 50,000 acres of these school lands, receiving ten per cent. of the certificates as my compensation for selecting them.

"An advance payment of ten cents per acre was required in gold, and the next question was how to get this gold safely to Madison. There were no railroads running through the State then; Beloit was the 'jumping-off place.' I procured a strong, old-fashioned hair trunk, filled it with layers of cotton batting, distributed my $6,500 of gold coin between the layers of cotton, locked it, put the key in my pocket, and surrounded the trunk with a complication of strong cords, with knots not easily untied. The weight of the trunk thus packed was not unusual, the light cotton and heavy coin averaging each other. Taking stage at Beloit, I saw my trunk strapped up behind the stage, and on arrival at Madison it was piled up with fifty others in the entry of the hotel, where it remained for more than three weeks, while I was away prospecting.

"I resolved to visit Bad Axe County. It was winter; the snow was deep and the air bleak and frosty. But I started out from Madison on horseback with a pocket compass in my saddlebags, and made my way down the Black Earth Valley to the Wisconsin River, and thence to Viroqua, through an unbroken forest. At Richland Centre I found a single log cabin, where I spent the night. From there to the Kickapoo River there were no roads. I made my way by pocket compass through the majestic forests. The only sign of human presence I came across was a deer hanging by his hind legs from a hickory sapling, having been shot and swung up by some hunter who took this method of preserving his meat from the wolves.

"At length I reached Viroqua. The news of my errand quickly spread, and one afternoon, on my return from prospecting, I heard that an indignation meeting of the inhabitants of the county was called, to meet at the shanty which served as a Court House, with the intention of putting a summary stop to my proceedings. I attended it, much to the surprise of some, who had called it, and asked for a hearing. I explained to the crowd that these lands, when sold, became at once subject to State and local taxation for roads, school houses, etc.; that they could only be made profitable to the buyers by reselling them, thus bringing in population and capital; in short, instead of a grasping speculator and greedy monopolist, I was a public benefactor. In this view I was supported by Mr. McMichael, the County Clerk. My arguments prevailed; a revulsion of feeling took place, a resolution of approval was adopted, and the meeting, designed to expel me, adjourned in an entirely good humor."

It was many years, however, before the lands thus acquired became profitable.

He first met Lucy Stone in 1850, when she called at his hardware store to cash a small check from the treasurer of the Anti-Slavery Society. He was so taken with her that he advised his elder brother Samuel, who was looking for a wife, to make her acquaintance; and he put off paying the check till the next day, in order to send Samuel to her with the money. Samuel, though he found her pleasing, was not moved to pay court to her; but the younger brother never forgot her. In 1853 he went east to attend the antislavery meetings of Anniversary Week. He heard Lucy speak in New York, and was filled with enthusiasm. A few days later, while listening to her plea for woman suffrage before a committee of the Massachusetts Constitutional Convention, he made up his mind to marry her if he could.

It took some courage even to think of such a thing. Although she was very popular with the abolitionists, the temperance people and the friends of woman's rights, she was looked upon by the conservative public as the embodiment of unwomanliness, and was denounced by the press as a "she-hyena." In reality, she was small and gentle, but gifted with entire courage, great natural eloquence, and a singularly sweet voice. Mobs would sometimes listen to her when they howled down every other speaker. He had a long and arduous courtship. Her mind was made up not to marry, and she had refused many offers; but she had never before been besieged by so charming and so formidable a wooer. "Your father could have got any woman to marry him," my mother's sister said to me, when she was herself a grandmother.

An incident of his antislavery work advanced him very much in Lucy's regard. When slaves were brought voluntarily by their owners into a free State, they became legally free. During an antislavery convention at Salem, O., while he was on the platform reciting a poem of his own composition, a telegram announced that the train going west through Salem at 6 P.M. would bring a little slave girl, with her master and mistress, on the way to Tennessee. A committee was appointed to take the child off the train, and did so. For his active part in this affair, he was fiercely abused by the press, a reward of $10,000 was offered for his head at a large public meeting in Memphis, Tenn., and, for months after, Kentuckians would come into his hardware store, look at him long and hard, and say, "Ah, damn you, we shall know you if we ever catch you on the other side of the river!" This hurt his business and angered his partners, but endeared him to Lucy.

Even after her heart was won, she felt that she ought to stay single, in order to devote herself wholly to her work for equal rights. But he promised to devote himself to the same work, and persuaded her that, together, they could do more for it than she could alone. No promise was ever more faithfully kept.

The reactionaries had often expressed the wish that some one would marry Lucy and "shut her up." A doggerel rhyme in the Boston *Post* closed with the lines:

> "A name like Curtius' shall be his,
> On Fame's loud trumpet blown,
> Who with a wedding kiss shuts up
> The mouth of Lucy Stone!"

But in after years the enemies of equal rights felt anything but gratitude towards my father. He added his own eloquent voice to hers, and together they made a great team.

The famous protest against the inequalities of the marriage laws, which they issued at the time of their wedding (May 1, 1855), was his idea, and was written by him, with suggestions from her. It had wide publicity, and helped to get the laws amended. He heartily concurred in her wish to keep her own name.

Harriet Beecher Stowe, who had known him for years as a young fellow full of fun, frolic and audacity, was amazed by his marriage to the serious and earnest woman's rights lecturer, seven years his senior. She said, "Is it possible that that wild boy has married Lucy Stone!"

One debt that I owed to my father was shared by the whole country. A comparatively small incident had great consequences. Public sentiment in Ohio in 1855 was about equally divided on the slavery question, but the free soilers were split into two factions, the Liberty party and the American party. Unless they could get together, they had no chance of defeating the pro-slavery men. A meeting held in Cincinnati to choose delegates was so stormy that union seemed hopeless, and the convention was about to break up in disorder, when, by an extraordinarily eloquent speech, he brought the two factions together, and secured the election of delegates favoring Salmon P. Chase. At the State Convention, the vote of the Cincinnati delegation turned the scale in favor of the nomination of Chase for Governor. A few years later, at the National Republican Convention, the vote of the Chase delegation turned the scale in favor of the nomination of Lincoln for President.

"We see dimly in the present what is small and what is
      great,
  Slow of faith, how weak an arm may turn the iron
      helm of fate."

Much of my childhood's happiness was owing to my father. He could spin fairy tales as enthralling as "Alice in Wonderland," making them up as he went along, with an unfailing flow of fancy. Some of them were serials, and ran for months. One was about a mermaid who had her nest in the reeds by the river. The eggs were square, pink at one end and purple at the other. She promised to reward him with three fairy gifts if he would come every night, for a certain length of time, and sit on the nest while she went away for rest and recreation. Her enemies were always trying to break the eggs. Sometimes they dropped down from the branches of the trees overhead; sometimes they came boring up through the nest from below. Sometimes they tried to make him late for his appointment. One evening a crowd of pigs got into the garden just as he was about to start. He chased them around and around, but they would not go out at the gate. At last it dawned upon him that they were goblin pigs, sent to delay him. He made a bee line for the river, arriving at the nest just in time. Once he was warned that some flour mills on his way had been set to grinding poisoned grain. Clouds of poisonous flour-dust came streaming out from the tall mills, and he had to make a long detour. Every night there was a fresh attack or a fresh stratagem—each a new delight to the little girl into whose eager ears the tale was poured.

During the nearly forty years of their married life, he worked side by side and hand in hand with his wife for the equal rights cause, getting up conventions, cir-

culating petitions, addressing Legislatures, and co-
operating in all the hard and heavy work of pressing an
unpopular reform. He helped to organize the New England Woman Suffrage Association in 1868, and the
American Woman Suffrage Association in 1869; he took
part in the campaigns for woman suffrage amendments
in many States, and helped the friends of equal rights
in many others to organize their State Associations.
His eloquence, wit, good humor and business ability
were a tower of strength to the movement. When Lucy
Stone raised the $10,000 with which the *Woman's
Journal* was started in Boston in 1870, with Mary A.
Livermore as editor, he gave her the first $1,000
towards it. He told her he would always help the paper
financially, but there was one thing he would never do,
and that was to take any part in the labor of editing it.
But later, when the $10,000 was all gone, and it became
necessary to have editors who would serve without pay,
he shouldered his share of that burden also, and con-
tinued to carry it as long as he lived, with such help as
I was able to give him and my mother later. For forty
years, he never missed attending the annual National
Conventions. The story of his manifold activities cannot
be told here. When Lucy Stone died, in 1893, he said to
me, "We must try to keep Mamma's flag flying"; and
during the sixteen years that he survived her, he never
ceased to work for it.

He was not only a champion of equal rights for all
women, but was a friend to any individual woman who
needed help, rich or poor, young or old, pretty or ugly;

he was always ready to lend a hand to help carry her burdens, literal or metaphorical.

He was a man of cosmopolitan sympathies. He was a member of the first society of American Friends of Russian Freedom, was an officer in the Friends of Armenia, and addressed innumerable protest meetings against the Armenian massacres, the massacres of the Jews in Russia, and the attempts to deport political exiles. The great foreign audiences stood up instinctively when he rose to speak. They looked upon him as the ideal American. At the celebration of his eightieth birthday, William Lloyd Garrison, the son of the Liberator, said:

"It is his virtue that the conduct of his special cause does not diminish his interest in every struggle for human freedom. He breaks a lance for all down-trodden and oppressed peoples. Wherever a protest against tyranny is called for, you may be sure that Mr. Blackwell will answer 'Adsum.' Tonight an Armenian meeting may claim his presence, tomorrow Russian exiles enlist his aid; if the Chinese are in the toils of persecution, he counts himself among their friends. When his fellow citizens rise against the coal monopoly, he is at Faneuil Hall to make the rousing speech of the occasion. When prejudice against the Negro and lynching horrors are to be denounced, his eloquent indignation is assured. . . . He abhors Imperialism, advocates with enthusiasm reciprocity and freer trade, is numerous at the State House committee hearings, to speak the humanitarian word on topics of wide diversity. Having finished his four-score years with juvenile freshness, he celebrates the beginning of his eighty-first year by helping organize a movement for the Initiative and Referen-

dum. How fortunate for us that he was early trans-
planted from English Bristol."

He was closely connected with the progress of women
in the professions. His elder sister, Dr. Elizabeth Blackwell, pioneered the way for women into medicine,
against tremendous opposition. When she died, at 89,
there were more than seven thousand women physicians
and surgeons in the United States. His sister-in-law, the
Rev. Dr. Antoinette Brown Blackwell, was the first
woman to be ordained a minister. She too was bitterly
denounced. When she died, at 96, more than three thousand women were preaching.

Not long before his death, some one said, in introducing him to a friend, "This gentleman is the husband of
Lucy Stone—or was the husband of Lucy Stone." "Is
the husband of Lucy Stone," he said, with an accent of
tenderness and pride.

He passed away on Sept. 9, 1909. He left directions
that his body should be cremated. He rather disliked
the idea of cremation, but he wished to follow his wife's
example, and to have their ashes mingled in one urn.
Dr. Borden P. Bowne, who conducted the funeral
service, said, in part:

"I do not know whether Mr. Blackwell belonged to
any church organization, and I am not much concerned
to know; but he belonged to the Church of churches,
the Church of the Good Samaritan. He loved righteousness and hated iniquity. He had a passion for justice,
and devoted his life to securing it. He lived with protest on his lips and with resistance in his will against

everything that harmed or hindered humanity. His individual benefactions were many, and generally wise. His life has been a blessing to multitudes. It would be hard to find another man so widely beloved. Social conditions are more just, laws are more equal, public morality has a higher tone, and the public conscience is more keen and discerning because of his life and work."

Even the attorney of the "Massachusetts Association Opposed to the Further Extension of Suffrage to Women," who had gibed and jeered at him at the legislative hearings for years, said after his death, "He was a splendid man." "Such a capable, wonderful man," a young business man remarked. "Such a wonderful, lovable man," said the editor of one of the chief Boston daily papers.

Of the many things that I owe to my father, the one for which I am most grateful is the example of a great and beautiful life.

To

CHARLES W. ELIOT

by

SAMUEL A. ELIOT

Arlington Street Church, Boston

The old rule that "children should be seen and not heard" did not prevail with us. . . .

* * * *

I see now why Father had such confidence in the verdict of youthful minds. . . .

* * * *

There was nothing dictatorial about him. . . .

* * * *

His mind was all daylight. There was no fogginess in his thought or speech.

SAMUEL A. ELIOT

It would be mighty convenient if one generation could start where the older generation leaves off and the world would get better and brighter more rapidly if that were the rule, but the creator does not seem to have arranged things that way. I cannot write much about "What I owe to my father" but I can say something of what I might have learned from my father if I had been sufficiently alert of mind and responsive of will.

My father early gave me to understand that a sound and serviceable body was essential for a happy and productive life. In his youth he had rowed in the Harvard Crew and from boyhood he had sailed boats, ridden horseback and taken long walks exploring the countryside. The fact that my mother and grandfather had both died of tuberculosis made him all the more eager that his boys should have every opportunity for out-of-door life and bodily exercise. So he saw to it that for ten years of my boyhood we spent the summers "camping out" in tents, usually on a lovely and uninhabited island on the coast of Maine. There one must needs learn to row, swim and sail, to chop, saw and lug wood, to fish and forage and to do the camp chores. There was, too, a comfortable sloop yacht in which we cruised the New England coast from New London to Eastport. We did not have firearms and I have never learned to enjoy hunting, and as that was long before

51

the days of motor boats and automobiles we learned
nothing about engines, but my father taught us, not by
precept, but by example or letting us learn by doing;
so that we could turn our hands to pretty much anything connected with the independent, self-reliant life
of the New England seacoast in those contentful though
comparatively primitive days.

In the winter-time horseback riding took the place
of sailing. My father rode horseback daily and there
was a pony for the boys. At that time the pleasant
suburbs of Boston were uncrowded and the roads soft
and safe for a small boy. Before I went to college I had
been encouraged to explore, on foot or on horseback,
most of eastern Massachusetts. I still feel that for
bodily thrills there is nothing to compare with steering
a lively yacht in a full-sail breeze or riding a powerful
horse across country at full speed. Both of these things
my father did well; and he was accustomed to expect
his boys to be competent and self-reliant.

Then, in the autumn there was football and in the
spring baseball and tennis. I never became a real expert in those healthy sports though I did captain my
school teams and got some invaluable experience in
leadership and in the merits of team play. I had my
share of bodily injuries which, I recall, my father
treated in too spartan a manner for my taste. His was a
"grin and bear it" attitude. I vividly remember how
once when as a small boy I fell overboard in very cold
water and in my fright swam after the boat with such
ferocious energy that my father laughed at me so hard

that he could hardly pull me aboard again. I was much offended. This does not mean that he was hard-hearted; probably he was delighted to discover that I could take care of myself in such an emergency. Anyway his boys were expected to have the physical hardihood and moral resolution to stand up to any reasonable knocks.

For intellectual training my father believed in the best and we were sent to schools of high repute and as a matter of course went to Harvard College. I did not take full advantage of these opportunities and indeed did not discover the real delights of the intellectual life until I was halfway through college and had the chance to select and pursue studies that really interested me. My father would look at me when I reported my poor standing, with a glance that was half derisive and half amused but never rebuked or lectured me. Reproof indeed would have gone off me like water off a duck's back. I was having a glorious time, singing in the Glee Club, acting in college dramatics, enjoying to the uttermost all the outside activities incident to college life and to light-hearted youth. I can see now that my father in no small degree sympathized with my more or less rebellious attitude toward the formal class exercises of those days. He was himself in the thick of the fight for educational reform and was going up and down the land denouncing the waste and misdirection and futility of much that was called Education. My record, which was the experience of many a normal, healthy-minded boy of good background, must have given him ammunition for his battles. If a boy of my fairly promising type

could not be interested in required Greek and solid
geometry why not let him study the things he did like
and which would kindle his ardor and awaken the in-
stinctive craving for knowledge? Anyway my real education up to my nineteenth year came mostly from
things outside of the school curriculum.

From childhood I was encouraged to browse among
my father's books. I do not think that my reading was
in any way "directed." There were the books, I took
what I liked. There were the histories of Parkman and
Prescott and MacCauley; the plays of Shakespeare, the
novels of Scott, Dickens, Thackeray and George Eliot,
the science of Darwin and Agassiz and Asa Gray, the
poetry of Shelley and Keats and Byron and the then
popular New England School, Lowell and Longfellow,
Holmes, Bryant and Whittier, all of whom were occasionally guests in my father's house. By the time I went
to college I was pretty widely read in English literature.
I was blind and deaf to the glories of the Greek and
Roman classics—they were associated with school tasks
—and I had not enough patience and application to enjoy foreign languages. I think I did read Dumas in
French but soon grew lazy and took to translations.
My chief quarrel with my father's plan, or lack of
plan, for my education is that he did not somehow insist
on my acquiring an adequate command of written and
spoken French and German. However, he undoubtedly
knew, as I know now, that "you can lead a boy to a
classroom but you can't make him think." My father
had no use for the education that consists in putting

information into a boy's mind as you would pack
articles in his trunk. The education that was worth
while was in what the boy acquired for himself, by the
wholesome exercise of his own capacities and the stimu-
lating force of his own aptitudes and ambitions.

I remember, too, how our scientific interests were
awakened and our observation quickened by competi-
tions in the collecting of minerals, shells and botanical
specimens. A walk always meant a lookout for queer
rock formations or unfamiliar trees and shrubs. Curiously enough birds were not included. My father was
very nearsighted so I suppose it was easier for him to
discuss trap dykes and glacial scratches than humming
birds. Then, too, on our coast cruises and land explora-
tions we were expected to read up the local histories
and legends and to note the characteristic industries.
We would talk whaling at Nantucket and sardines at
Eastport, fishing at Gloucester, lumbering at Bangor,
ship building at Bath, lime burning at Rockland and
old New England history at Plymouth, Provincetown,
Castine and Pemaquid. All these studies have proved
lifelong sources of enjoyment.

Another form of education was in the "table talk,"
and there my father's practice differed from that of
most of the families in which I visited or with whose
habits I became acquainted. The old rule "children
should be seen but not heard" did not prevail with us.
Even when there were distinguished guests at table the
boys were expected to take their share in the conversation or, at least, to be interested in something more than

the things to eat. Public affairs, college business, scientific discoveries, new inventions, were discussed not only before us but with us. It was assumed that we read the daily paper and the best of the weekly periodicals and our opinions were both asked and expressed about current events. My father was an animated interrogation point and sought information from every source and angle. He was a good listener and gave equal attention to the argument of the statesman and a child's story of the day's adventures. He gave an unusual deference to the judgments of young people. I suspect that his decisions in regard to the merits of Deans and Professors were more often based on the estimates of students than of colleagues. To students a teacher was likely to be either "bum" or "bully" and that verdict, if supported by valid testimony, carried weight with the President. Naturally in the forty years of his Presidency of Harvard my father had as his guests many men and women of renown in the academic world and in the realms of politics, business, science, art and literature. With these people and about them my brother and I had spirited discussions and formed rather impetuous opinions. As the people I thus met in my youth become historic characters I find those early formed prejudices—for or against—still at the back of my mind and am often surprised to find how time has justified and confirmed them. After all the vision of youth is likely to be lucid and disinterested. The mirror is as yet untarnished. I see now why my father had such confidence in the verdict of youthful minds on people or

events and why he would often change the whole tone
of some speech or article he was writing after reading
it to a grandchild and both inviting and getting a frank
comment or criticism.

But the influence of a man is not just in what he says
or does but in what he is. Character is singularly con-
tagious. A man's way of looking at things inevitably
affects those who come in contact with him. Except at
sea, when orders must be promptly obeyed, my father
seldom issued commands. There was nothing dictatorial
about him. He would seldom tell a child "Do this" or
"Don't do that." He led but did not drive. He reasoned
and explained but did not coerce or overpower. He
never punished me by the use of superior strength.
He had the courage to let me try dangerous things,
knowing that "a burnt child dreads the fire." Yet one
never had any hesitation in determining what he desired
and expected. Courtesy and ready sympathy, joined
with a frankness of speech that seemed to some people
inconsiderate, marked all his social intercourse. His
dignity and reserve were a fireproof curtain to bore-
some or impertinent people, but tenderness and deep
affections irradiated all his family life. He did not
possess the expansive and demonstrative quality that is
essential to a certain kind of popularity. He could not
wear his heart on his sleeve. He was deficient in the
bantering jocularity which sometimes passes for good
fellowship. His speech was neither jocose nor satirical.
He had a poor memory for jests but he was able to
laugh at other people's jokes and thoroughly to enjoy

the caricatures of his own manners and speeches in which his grandchildren excelled.

His mind was all daylight. There was no fogginess in his thought or speech. He raised no false hopes. He made no veiled promises. His vocabulary consisted of plain serviceable words. He wore no rhetorical flowers in his buttonhole. His public addresses may have lacked color and humor but they had weight and persuasive force. They were distinguished for terseness, precision and breadth of comprehension. He understated rather than overestimated his case. In writing he could be as compact as one of the Essays of Bacon that lay on his study table. He hated cant, had no use for artful stratagems, disliked bombastic display and self-glorification.

But it was the general attitude of his mind and spirit even more than his spoken and written words that inspired confidence and carried conviction. The indirect and unintended influence was the most enduring. It was the influence of one who was absolutely disinterested and to whom the world could offer no bribes. He saw clearly, thought independently and willed nobly. He touched public affairs with a lifting power. Politics was not to him a game or a business but a matter of intelligent patriotism. For two generations his fellow-citizens looked to him for an interpretation of public questions which though not always popular was sure to be candid and impartial. They trusted his insight and foresight. He was a kind of conscience for the political world, quick to expose incompetency or rebuke corruption but readier to believe in honesty and sincerity. He brought to the consideration of public questions a knowledge of past and contemporary experiments in government, an inflexible confidence in democracy, a contempt for mean deceptions and self-seeking intrigues, a love of fair play and the detachment of a man interested not so much in party triumphs as in the progress of freedom, justice and goodwill.

My father was also able to communicate to his sons and to those about him the optimism which characterizes people who believe in the sovereignty of a good and just God. His religious faith was simple but profound and sufficient. It was the mainspring of his private life and of his public endeavors. He did not say much about his religion but he lived it. Christianity was to him not a system of doctrine or a sacred ritual, but a way of life. He was a regular and devout churchgoer—usually twice on Sundays and always at the daily morning prayers in the College Chapel. He taught his boys religion not by precept or catechism but chiefly by hymns and poetry. Before I was twelve years old I knew by heart most of the hymns in the Chapel hymnbook of that time and later when I sang in the College Choir I seldom had occasion to look at the book for both words and tunes were familiar. In the family life the day often began with a hymn, for all the family sang. What he wrote of my brother might be said of my father, "He believed that a loving God rules the universe, that the path to loving and serving Him lies through loving and serving men, and that the way to worship Him is to reverence the earthly beauty, truth and goodness He has brought forth." That faith gave him serenity and good cheer through all the sorrows and disappointments of life. It made him "always young for liberty." It sustained him in every fight against stupidity, cruelty and wrong and invigorated him in all his efforts to advance noble human causes.

To

WILLIAM FILENE

by

EDWARD A. FILENE

Boston

Without learning from my father that straight
thinking should be substituted for traditional
thinking, such business success as I have achieved
would not have been possible.

EDWARD A. FILENE

My father was not an extraordinary man as to where he arrived, but he was extraordinary in the distance he advanced. Although he died more than twenty-five years ago, not a day passes without my thinking of him.

I learned these three great truths from my father:

1. To endeavor to think clearly so that today I can write honestly and unsentimentally about him.

2. To disbelieve in miracles—whether ancient or modern—and from that I learned that success of any kind was to be paid for just as surely as is a railroad ticket or a suit of clothes.

3. By his example, to bear pain uncomplainingly.

Let me try to analyze the value of these teachings.

In the past, filial love has been deified. This is entirely human and natural. It is common among animals, but it is more marked among human beings because it became basically essential when humanity emerged from primitive life into higher forms. Each advance in civilization was accomplished with difficulty. There was constant danger of recession, especially among the young and weak. Without the parent's love for his child and the constant guidance of the parent, the child might often have lost ground and lapsed into more primitive forms.

With the unquestioned right of the parent to hold

property and acquire special privileges came also a tendency to accord to the parent superior thinking powers. The idea has grown until it is believed that it is a son's duty personally to regard and describe his father to others as relatively perfect and as youth's perfect example. In reality, a father is no different from you or me. He is a mixture of strength and weakness, and of good and bad thinking or action.

The world has been immeasurably retarded and hurt by well-meant but irrational deification of parents. This has led not only to out-of-date traditional thinking, but also to youth's discouragement because youth is thus made to believe that successful men are successful because they have inherited qualities which youth may not have inherited and consequently cannot possess.

As I write, I am certain of one thing—that is, that my father would feel he had utterly failed in his teaching if, on account of my love for him, I lied about him and thereby harmed the world he tried to help onward.

Belief in miracles belittles our ideas of God. An omniscient and omnipotent God requires no miracles. I have become more and more theistic as I perceive that natural law was adequate at the beginning of things and is still as adequate after millions of years of evolution. By discrediting miracles, I have learned to depend on natural law.

I have learned that to achieve success, I must pay the full price in kind for it, which usually means not money, but rather straight thinking, hard work, and good health. When I have failed, it has usually been because I was too weak to pay the full price and not because I had not analyzed what the price would be.

It is to this kind of thinking which my father taught me that I owe whatever business success I have achieved. I found the retail business, in which I have spent my life, organized and managed largely on tradition. I found in it, both directly and indirectly, enormous wastes. By applying fact-finding methods rather than a belief in miracles or traditional methods, I have made many changes in retailing that have on the whole proved successful. Without learning from my father that straight thinking should be substituted for traditional thinking, such business success as I have achieved would not have been possible.

To

FRANK S. FOSDICK

by

HARRY EMERSON FOSDICK

The Riverside Church, New York

His teaching was to him a ministry and his school office a confessional. . . .

*   *   *   *

He did not propose, he said, to let the younger generation get ahead of him: he intended to keep one jump ahead of it.

HARRY EMERSON FOSDICK

My grandfather, as a little child, arrived in Buffalo in a covered wagon after a three weeks' trip across New York State. He was in his young manhood, an artisan working at cobbling and carpentering, and, passionate for an education, he learned the declinations of Latin nouns and the conjugation of Latin verbs as he worked at his bench. Later, having taught school in Buffalo for over forty years, he ended as Superintendent of Education of the city.

My father taught in the schools of Buffalo for over fifty years. He had had under his instruction so many of the city's youths and he was so affectionately regarded by them that, when I walked down the street with him in his later years, it was almost as easy to keep my hat off altogether as to be so continuously lifting it in answer to the salutations. His teaching was to him a ministry and his school office a confessional. Every kind of trouble that boys and girls know, from love affairs and economic difficulties to moral struggles and religious problems, came to his room. He carried his students on the shoulders of his personal care with an affection that brought its rich reward in answering gratitude.

This was all the reward he sought. He lived on the narrow means of a school teacher, and it was often difficult to make ends meet, but he would not have done anything else. In all my boyhood I do not recall that the idea of living for the sake of making money ever occurred to me. That was a conception of life so alien to our home that it was not credible. To make the most of one's self for the sake of others, to become in some useful realm a skilled workman—this from the first was the assumed ideal, and anything else would have been unthinkable.

This is a basic thing my father did for me, not by what he said but by the whole tenor and spirit of his life. Money-making was precluded as an end in living and skilled service was exalted as the one durable satisfaction and worthwhile goal.

My father inherited from his father an ardent spirit of independence. They were both old-fashioned Americans with the attitude of the pioneers not yet extinguished in them. They both had unregimented minds, and in practical affairs they resented nothing so much as restriction on their liberty. I have heard my father say many a time that if anybody ever told him he must not do something that was the very thing he proposed to do.

This spirit entered into their religion and made the Baptist churches with their autonomous, independent congregations, their refusal of creedal subscription, and their insistence on the competence of the individual soul in matters of faith, congenial to their temperament. This same spirit made them ardent foes of slavery. My grandfather's home was one of the last stations on the Underground Railroad, and my father

used to recall stormy nights when a tap on the window-
pane would wake his sire to go out into the night and
row escaping slaves across the Niagara River to
Canada and freedom. One slave hidden in a secret
closet in my grandfather's home died of fright while
the pursuers were searching the premises to find him.
My boyhood's home was saturated with this insistence
on freedom for the individual, with this sympathy for
and indignation about every oppressed under-dog.

This love of independence my father carried over
into his school. He distrusted rules. He refused to
govern by prohibitions. That every boy was to be a
gentleman and every girl a lady was a summary I once
heard him make of the only rule he wanted in his
school. To be sure, when some unappreciative and
fractious youth tried to take advantage of his trust,
impose on him, and ride him, my father could create
on call a thunderstorm of indignation that was posi-
tively terrifying. Once was enough for any student or
any son of his to face that outburst. Few ever ven-
tured it a second time. But the efficiency of his indignation lay in the very fact that he was tirelessly working to make boys and girls independent of rules, with
their conduct inwardly determined, not outwardly imposed, and, knowing that, they knew that they were
on their honor to play fair.

This was the method which my father used in the
training of his own children, and for it I can never be
sufficiently grateful. Today I read modern psychologists
proclaiming their new methods of rearing children with

some amusement at the word "new." At any rate, if
they are new, my father was far ahead of his time.
He was not possessive. His one idea was to train us for
competent independence in our judgment and life. To
this end he ran the home democratically, and among
my earliest recollections are invitations to join family
conferences and to contribute my childish opinion on
some general question needing decision, as though
already I were counting as a copartner in the management of the family. He seldom made autocratic decisions; he called the family group together and made
us children his conferees. It was wonderful training.
The spirit which it created developed a family loyalty
stronger than steel. As for our attitude toward him, it
produced a compelling love and admiration. He was
always our chum. We did things together. He respected our personalities. When we asked his judgment he tossed the question back again and made us
think through the matter for ourselves. He wanted no
rubber stamps among his children. Yes-yessing was
his *bête noire*. And I doubt if any father in the world
ever knew with quicker sensitiveness just when to keep
his hands entirely off and let us steer ourselves.

His corrective methods, in retrospect, seem to me
full of this kind of wisdom. At one notable time, when
post-adolescent rebellions were making me a rather un-
manageable member of the family, my father did a
characteristic thing—took me off alone with him for a
day's fishing. He used to do that occasionally, both for
the fun of it and for the use he could make of it. He

knew how much more effective playing with a boy is than upbraiding him. To this day I can remember in detail what he said to me on that special day's fishing, how neatly he worked it in while we were catching perch, how easy it was to take it from him under those circumstances, how deep down it went, and how much good it did.

Asked to write on what my father did for me, I cannot separate him from my mother. They were one. Never in all my boyhood did they fail to stand together on any question which affected the children. We never could play one off against the other, or find anywhere a rift between them. I recall yet the impression made upon me when in my early childhood my father said to me that even the Virgin Mary, so it seemed to him, could not have been lovelier than my mother was. In brief, my father and my mother loved each other and there was peace at home. While my mother for years was a semi-invalid and my father had at least one serious breakdown from over-work, and the financial struggle to educate their children was exceedingly difficult, always beneath the stress and anxiety of special crises we knew that the home itself was as secure as the orbits of the stars.

I read these current disquisitions on trial marriage and extra-marital relationships with an impervious mind. I pity the people whose experience with family life is such that the best they can say about it makes it a loose, tentative, irresponsible relationship intolerable without other liaisons. Such views of marriage do not spring from intelligence but from unhappy experience, just as my firm belief in monogamy springs not from argument but from an experience so fortunate that I know where great living lies. A home such as I was reared in is the most beautiful human relationship on earth.

Together my father and mother gave me religion. I caught it from them, for they both were deeply religious. Their theology was by tradition evangelical, but it never was narrowly sectarian nor theologically constricted. When I came home from college at the end of my Freshman year I had a bombshell in hand with which to blow up the household. I believed in evolution. I saved the announcement for the psychological moment when its repercussion would have the greatest effect. My father heard me through and then when I had exhausted my statement of this new and revolutionary light on my mind he said quietly, "I believed in evolution before you were born."

As the years passed my father never stopped growing in his religious thinking. He did not propose, he said, to let the younger generation get ahead of him; he intended to keep one jump ahead of it. But whether with the old set of opinions that belonged in the family background or with the newer formulations which came to be confidently his, he was a religiously-minded man. He used frankly to bring religion into his public school assemblies and, so far as I know, neither Jew, Catholic, nor Protestant objected. His was a practically operative faith, free from partisanship, concerned about integrity of character and social service, and what he said about it his own life illustrated.

In the home I can recall yet the freedom with which he treated religion, his impatience with its shams, his independence of its bigotries and prejudices, his breadth of tolerance. Yet always I recall, too, the impression of religious reality and reverence which his life carried with it. If, through the upsets and turmoils of a generation whose rapid changes have stripped so many of their faith, I have kept my assurance that while religions pass religion abides, I have most of all to thank what I experienced in my boyhood's home.

To

MARCUS MORTON HOLMES

by

JOHN HAYNES HOLMES

The Community Church, New York

The clearest memory of my father seems to attach itself to our evenings at home. . . .

* * * *

He haunted the library, pored over newspapers and magazines, and began out of his scanty earnings to buy books. . . .

* * * *

If there is any one thing which I most like to recall in connection with my father, it is that he grew throughout his life.

JOHN HAYNES HOLMES

I HAVE been trying to remember the first time that I discovered my father. I cannot recall that I knew him at all in our first home in Philadelphia where I lived during the first years of my life. There seem to rise up in my mind a few pictures of my second home in Everett, Massachusetts, where I lived until my seventh year, but outlines are dim and persons mere shadows on a screen. The first distinct memories seem to be associated with my home in Malden, Massachusetts, where I lived until I went to college. Perhaps it is because this home was a definite part of my life over a long and later period of time, as the first homes were not, that I can here see my father clearly. In any case, I discover him now, within the realm of memory, as he walked up the hill from the railroad station after the trip home from Boston on the suburban train, as he mowed the lawn or picked the peaches in our yard, as he and my mother gathered us children together on a Sunday morning and escorted us regularly to church and Sunday school. Is it because as children we take our parents for granted, because father and mother are so integral a part of the earliest landscape we see, that we seem to discover them as distinctive objects in our lives rather later than we do other and less familiar realities? I wonder!

The clearest memory of my father seems to attach itself to our evenings at home. Evenings in those days were different from what they are today. Outside distractions were few. We stayed at home and gathered around the kerosene lamp because, among other things, there was nothing else to do. There were no theatres nearer than Boston, five miles away, no movie shows, no automobile excursions. Occasionally there was a children's party, a visit to the neighbors, or a sociable at the church. In the winter time there was coasting on the hill and skating on the pond under the bright starlight, and in the summer there were occasional jaunts to Revere Beach and to the woods in Middlesex Fells. But ordinarily, both summer and winter, we stayed at home. Even here, inside the home, there were few of the distractions and entertainments that we have today. Thus there was no radio, nor even telephone, to remind us of the outer world. The music box was a substitute for the talking machine, but a poor substitute, and, its tunes exhausted, lay silent most of the time. Card games were a frequent source of amusement. Backgammon, an amazing new discovery of today, was a familiar resource. But the chief solace of the long hours after supper, when the lamp was lit on the center table, was reading. And here my father was our "guide, counsellor and friend."

My father had little education as a boy. Born on a farm in the Bridgewater district south of Boston, he did the chores, and played with his comrades, and picked up such training as he could in the district school. By the time he was in his early 'teens he was

finding his way to Boston and earning his living. To the
end of his days he showed the meagerness of his early
education in his bad spelling and his occasional slips
of grammar. But deep in my father's heart, as inherited
from a long succession of Puritan ancestors, was a love
of learning and an appreciation of the fine things in
human life. When he journeyed to Boston as a mere
lad, to support himself and to live on his own, he gravi-
tated naturally to the best instead of the worst asso-
ciates. He attended the old First Universalist Church,
and was busy in its parish activities. He found his way
into the upper gallery of the Boston Museum, and saw
night after night the notable productions of the famous
stock company of that historic theatre. He haunted the
library, pored over newspapers and magazines, and
began out of his scanty earnings to buy books. When
I came to intellectual consciousness as a boy, and began
to read, I found a small but excellent selection of volumes which my father had gathered one by one in the
years of his youth and early manhood. Here were two
or three works of Thackeray, a copy or two of Dickens's novels, some Whittier, Longfellow and Bryant,
some collections of sermons, and a strange array of
the writings of Swedenborg. I remember also some
paper-covered volumes stowed away in the attic, which
included tales by Charles Kingsley and George Eliot,
and Olive Shreiner's "Story of an African Farm."
Later, as a gift from the publisher, an old friend of
the family, came a set of Chambers' Encyclopædia.
First, among all these books, however, at least in my

father's affection, were some plays of Shakespeare. My
father was a lover of books all his days and had an
almost infallible gift of discrimination in his literary
selections. He seemed to find his way easily and naturally to the classics and to the best writing of his own
time. Among all the great novelists of the Victorian era,
George Eliot was his favorite. Long before Thomas
Hardy was known, except as a popular novelist, my
father recognized his genius, and proclaimed him in
season and out as the greatest literary genius of modern
times. I have always been sorry that my father did not
live to see his favorite, for whom he fought many a
good battle in his time, buried with world honors in
Westminster Abbey.

My love of books, one of the central passions of my
life, sprang from my father's love of books as a great
bough springs from the trunk of a tree. The mere
presence in our sitting room of the little library which
my father gathered at such cost and treasured with
such care, stirred within my heart a prime interest in
literature for its own sake. As I now gaze around my
collection of books, with its some eight or nine thousand volumes, I can see as it were a forest grown from
the little group of saplings which my father planted.
But these few volumes, always given a place of honor
in our modest home, were surely a secondary influence
as compared with the inspiration which came from
their possessor. For my father always delighted, in
his prime, to read aloud. He had studied elocution, and
for a few years had been a professional actor. It was

on the stage itself that he had first learned to love the plays of Shakespeare. I have always felt that he would have liked to have remained an actor to the end of his days, or perhaps have been a preacher or a public orator. His fine natural abilities as a reader and speaker would have served him well and brought him great success. But the stern economic necessities of his life bound him to the wheel of labor, and he could not escape before it was too late. It was something of a comfort to him, I think, to take a volume off of the bookshelves on a winter evening, and read aloud to the family. I can hear today the fine fervor of his voice, his impeccable sense of rhythm, and his noble response to eloquence and beauty. It was at his feet, so to speak, that I first caught my love of poetry and first learned my appreciation of its tonal values. What my father read to us I do not know, but my first recollection seems to be of "Evangeline." Then naturally came "The Courtship of Miles Standish" and "Hiawatha." Scenes from Shakespeare's plays were always in order, and I became familiar with the great passages in "Hamlet," "Macbeth," "Julius Cæsar," long before I was able to know what they meant or where they were. In due time, of course, I learned to read, and found satisfaction in selecting my own books and poring over their pages by myself. One of my earliest adventures was Scott, which kindled a fire which has never been extinguished. The verses of "Marmion" set me all aflame, and I was not satisfied until I had read all of Scott's poetry, then raced through the "Waverley Novels," and at last read Lockhart's six volumes of the famous biography. I had exhausted the bulk of the Scott literature before my third year in High School. But from this time on, books have been my constant companions day and night, at home and abroad. I like to feel that my experience with literature began as the experience of the race began—with the hearing of the spoken word as chanted by one who knew its worth and beauty. My father was the minstrel of my early days.

If the first and greatest influence that came to me from my father's life was surely in the field of literature, the second and perhaps more important influence was as surely in the field of religion. I often wonder if my experience with my parents in the church-going of my boyhood is not an answer to the question as to why the young people of our time are no longer interested in the church. Are not these young people the spiritual as well as the physical descendants of their fathers and mothers? Is it not true that they are indifferent to religion not so much because they have lost their interest in the church as because they never acquired an interest which was lost by their parents before they ever came upon the scene?

Fifty years ago, of course, there was nothing to do on Sunday but go to church. People flocked to religious services quite as much for social as for spiritual reasons, and in the friendly gatherings in the meeting-house found the great diversion and entertainment of the day. Church-going, that is to say, was the established way of occupying the hours of the Sabbath. But my father and mother were both interested in the church for other and more definite reasons. My father was himself very much of a free-thinker. He had done considerable reading in the theological and historical field, and had quite emancipated himself from the trammels of ecclesiastical convention both in thought and in conduct. He had his own ideas on religious questions, and these more frequently than not ran counter to the ideas of the established churches. Nevertheless, my father went to church regularly. In the first town which I can remember, he attended the Universalist church, located about a half-mile from our home upon the hill. In Malden, Massachusetts, he identified himself with the Unitarian church, which in this town was not at the top but at the bottom of the hill. Occasionally, when I was a boy, more frequently as I grew older, he would take me to Boston on a Sunday to hear some one of the distinguished preachers of the day. For long we planned to go to Trinity church on some great day and hear Phillips Brooks. But, alas, this modern Chrysostom was made Bishop of his diocese, and thus taken out of the pulpit; and fifteen months later he died almost without warning. So we never heard him. But Minot J. Savage, Edward Everett Hale, and others, were heard often. I recall one exciting Sunday evening at the old Boston Theatre, when we sat enthralled by the eloquence of Robert G. Ingersoll.

These Sunday excursions to the city convinced me that my father's primary interest in the church was in the preaching. He loved great preaching exactly as he

loved great acting. The spoken word brought to him a
kind of spell which captured him utterly. As I think of
his own untrained but rare oratorical gifts, I am
tempted to believe that he never heard a fine preacher
without putting himself in the preacher's place and
dreaming that he might have been a clergyman himself
had chance been with him rather than against him. In
any case, he was a faithful listener, one of the ablest
sermon-tasters I have known; and as I usually accompanied him on his Sunday morning excursions, his passion for the spoken word became my own as well. Fur-
thermore, my father always loved people, and liked
nothing better than to find himself in a friendly gathering of men and women. Great reader though he was,
he preferred the living person to the printed page,
and companionship was the joy of his life. I have
known him on a railroad trip, to walk the length of
the train with shining eyes in the hope of finding some
friend or acquaintance with whom he could share the
pleasures of the journey. So a church gathering was to
him a welcome occasion. He joined happily in the worship because it was an expression of human fellowship,
and lingered long after the service because there was a
chance to talk over the sermon and the affairs of the
day with his neighbors. My father was not devout—I
sometimes think that the monthly social at the church
with its baked beans and rolls and pie meant quite as
much to him as the more solemn occasion on Sunday
morning. His religion, apart from the intellectual challenge of thought and speculation, was basically a re-

ligion of fellowship. He would have appreciated William Morris's lines, which I am sure he never knew: "Fellowship is life, and lack of fellowship is death; fellowship is heaven, and lack of fellowship is hell; and the things which ye do upon the earth, it is for fellowship's sake that ye do them."

My father's influence was predominant in stirring my own interest in religion and the church. Down to the time I went to college, this interest was large and deep. It involved regular attendance at the church on Sunday mornings, long association with the Sunday school, and frequently a service or meeting on Sunday evening. Later came intense activity in the young people's society in the church. As a lad I always spoke my piece at the Sunday school festivals, and later, as a young man, I frequently read papers or gave short addresses before the gathering of young men and women. In all this my father had interest and gave encouragement. On going to college, however, there came a sudden change in my experience. The first two years at Harvard seemed to constitute a period of escape. I had left my home, and must now prove my independence by breaking the habits and conventions of my life. So I did not attend the college chapel, and broke all religious contacts of any kind. But the planting of my early days was deep, and the seeds were bound sooner or later to sprout and break the surface of the ground. By the time of my junior year in college, I was leading a Sunday school in Cambridge, and when I became a senior I announced to my classmates, as I had already announced to my family, that I had decided to become a minister. I cannot recall that my father ever persuaded me to make this choice of a profession. I search my mind in vain for any recollection of even a word from him on this subject. I think he had a great reverence for my own integrity as a person, and had no desire to intrude upon a matter which belonged so intimately to myself. But it is not difficult to recall his warm expression of pleasure when I told him of my decision, and one of the happiest memories of my life is that of his enthusiasm and pride to the end of his days over what I was doing in the ministry. There never was a man whose mind was freer than his, never a man who had less reverence for the church as such, never a man less given to piety. My father was a non-conformist to the very marrow of his bones. Yet by the unconscious influence of his own example he led his oldest son straight into the professional practice of religion.

My father's independence of thought in things religious brings me to a third and very impressive influence which he exerted upon my life. It was from him more than any other one source, I believe, that I learned the lesson of thinking through my own problems, of reaching my own conclusions, and of standing by my own convictions however much alone and at whatever cost. The fact that my father attended Universalist and Unitarian churches in communities which were prevailingly orthodox, and that he sought out great preachers of all faiths without prejudice, showed clearly enough his courage and self-reliance. But this

fact made no great impression upon my mind, as I was
not aware until much later of the emotions that run
rampant in the religion. So it was in the political rather
than in the religious world that I first learned from
my father's example what it meant to fight the good
fight for one's own ideals.

I was five years old when in 1884 the Cleveland-
Blaine election contest convulsed the nation. Memories
attached to the campaign are the first which I can seem
to recognize within my mind. The great torchlight pro-
cession, for example, which swept through the streets
of Boston on one of the last nights of the campaign,
burns as brilliantly in my mind today as it did in the
chill November air of Boston forty-six years ago. I can
still see those unending lines of flaming torches, and the
huge transparency of James G. Blaine which my grandfather hung upon the front of his home on Columbus
Avenue. But this furious political struggle sticks in my
mind not only because of such dramatic events in the
outer world which shook me as a youngster with a kind
of exquisite terror, but also because of the fierce con-
tention which shook my family like an earthquake in
its inner councils. For all the members of the family,
male and female, with the exception of two, were ferocious Republicans. They regarded Blaine as the bright
palladin who led the hosts of Heaven, and Cleveland as
a black Beelzebub who had been vomited up from the
nether regions to lead the hosts of Hell. All would have
been peaceful within the family, apart from the furore
that broke into the home from the distracted nation

outside, had it not been for the two black sheep in the white Republican fold. The first of these, the older man, was my grandfather's brother. After a life-long fidelity to Republicanism, he had decided to vote for Cleveland. But he was an amiable man, who was much more inclined to laugh than to shout over political disputes, and who therefore quite refused to defend his hero and battle for his cause. The other exception was my father, who was good-natured enough, but who had found in his admiration for Grover Cleveland one of the profound experiences of his life and was therefore as fierce in advocacy of this candidate as my grandfather and other members of the family were fierce in his denunciation. My father, in other words, unlike my great-uncle, drew his sword, and with his sword drew blood. I was young at the time, so young that events slipped away from my mind much oftener than they were retained. But I can remember to this hour, and shall remember to my dying day, the disputes which split the welkin of my grandfather's home as the Cleveland-Blaine campaign raged on to its cataclysmic conclusion. Always I saw my father fighting alone. The whole family was pursuing him, hot with wrath and hungry for vengeance. I can understand today that my father's attitude involved a certain treason to the family tradition, and thus deserved outlawry if not death itself. But my father, while never losing patience, never gave way an inch. It was word for word, argument for argument, blade-stroke for blade-stroke, with the family always shrilly victorious from sheer force of num-

bers, if nothing more. Intuitively my heart went out
in loyal sympathy to my father. The five scant years
of my age still made me old enough to sense the sig-
nificance of his fight. Now that time has passed, and all
the storm of those days has swept away, I can judge
Grover Cleveland and his place in history with cool
detachment. I feel that the hot partisans of that day
were deceived and that no great issues were involved in
that memorable campaign. I am convinced that Cleveland himself was opposed to those currents of thought
and life which have in this later age swept me into their
stream. But to this day I thrill to the mention of Cleveland's name, and soberly regard him as one of the ablest
and bravest of our Presidents. And this opinion springs
from the courage of this rugged man in fighting for
what he believed against every opposition however
strong and however certain of triumph, which courage
I saw anticipated, and for me made real, in my father's
championship of Cleveland's cause against enormous
odds. Right there and then I learned what it means to
have the courage of one's convictions, and how again
and again the whole duty of life is summed up in the
obligation to stand by these convictions. By no studied
precept but by his own unconscious personal example,
my father taught me this early in my life, and again
and again at many a later time, the duty of maintaining
the integrity of one's own mind. I know of no more important lesson. Dull conformity generation after generation, age after age, is the curse of our race. To break
this chain of custom, and to think and act for one's self

alone, is the highest service that one can render to society.

I think of one rather dramatic instance of my father's independence and whole-hearted fidelity to conviction which is of special interest perhaps because of certain of the circumstances of our own time. My father was a stern opponent of liquor and the liquor traffic. By conviction and practice he was a total-abstainer. No alcoholic beverages were ever allowed to come into our house, for he believed that the use of such beverages was an unforgivable offense against public decency and social welfare. The liquor traffic in our home was a moral question, and so it has remained in my life down to the present moment. Now it happened on a certain day that I was seriously ill with some kind of a throat trouble. The physician who came to my bedside in the morning, after my father had gone to work, prescribed among other things some wine for the cleansing and easing of my flaming throat. The wine was promptly procured and the bottle placed upon the table by my bed. In the evening my father returned home and came immediately to my room to see me. As he entered, he saw the amazing spectacle of a wine-bottle.

"What's that?" he said.

"Why," said my mother, "that's some wine that Dr. Nordstrom ordered for John's throat."

Without a word my father marched to the table, seized the wine-bottle, opened a window and threw the bottle into the yard. This father of mine meant business on the liquor question. He would no more tolerate it than he would tolerate slavery, or prostitution, or the drug traffic, or any other social abomination. How he would hoot if he were alive today at the sophistries and hypocrisies of the "wet" crowd that is now demoralizing the nation! He knew that the only way to get rid of liquor is to destroy it, every drop, and refuse to tolerate it under any specious plea. I learned that night, sick as I was, that "no compromise" is the slogan of every good fight, and that no victory ever yet was won by parleying with the enemy.

In trying to assess my father's influence upon my life, I think of one more thing. This is not so much a direct line of influence in itself as a certain atmosphere or environment in which my father lived and necessarily made his family live. I have already referred to my father's appreciation of fine things, and more specifically, to his love of literature, of the theatre, and of culture generally. He wanted to be an actor; he would have been a highly successful minister, he might have been an important political leader. He had a good mind, a courageous spirit, a high gift of oratory, and an unimpeachable character. But he never had any training which fitted him for any of these specialized tasks. He therefore drifted into business. When I first woke up to his existence, he was the head of a wholesale furniture house which occupied a loft on Portland Street in Boston. I can remember going into this loft, and seeing the vast array of chairs, sofas and tables which filled it from end to end, and threading my way as through a forest to a little partitioned office in the rear where my father had his desk side by side with his bookkeeper. My father always seemed distraught to me in this place, and I can see now that he was never happy there. Some years later than my earliest memories, his business failed, and he went "on the road" for some other whole-sale furniture dealer. His later life developed other vicissitudes in the business world. The fact is, he was never a success as a business man, and the reason was that he hated business, detested it, loathed it. It offered nothing to answer to the appeals of his nature. It satis-fied not a single interest in his life. While selling, he was thinking of politics or religion. While footing up accounts, he was dreaming of the book he was reading or the play he was soon to see. I cannot recall that my father was ever successful in fastening his mind on bus-iness affairs. This brought disaster to our home, and the margin of comfort was at times pretty low. But my father could not make a "go" of it because, from the high standards of his life, he *would* not make a "go" of it. This was not his world, and he more or less un-consciously refused to live in it.

I think I learned from my father's experience, and from the troubles that his business disasters brought into our home, to hate business even as he did. My grandfather was a highly successful business man, and I admired him as one of the heroes of my boyhood life; but his business was music, and music seemed in his case to save the situation. Business just for its own sake very early appeared to me to be unworthy, and, for my father's sake, if nothing more, I wanted nothing to do with it. I can remember a time in my life when I was sorely tempted to give up college and go into my grandfather's business, but it was the music which drew me and not the business itself, for this was at the time when I was attending the concerts of the Boston Symphony Orchestra and of the Kneisel Quartette, and was beginning to learn the wonders of opera. But this aberration soon vanished and when I went to college, I knew that I must enter one of the great professions. More immediately than my father ever knew, the failure of his business life was the influence that carried me through college, through the theological school, into the ministry, and thus into all the success and happiness that I may have tasted in my life.

It comforts me to remember that the chief comfort of my father's last years came from his delight in my work and in that of my brother, a successful lawyer. Paralyzed nine years before his death, he would sit in his chair and receive us boys gladly as we came to him from time to time and shared with him the experiences of our professional work. I am sure that I am right when I yield to the belief that my father saw in me and in my brother something of what he had wanted all his life to be himself. I think he felt that his own life had been much of a failure—that he had really never had the opportunity to do anything that he had wanted to do. But there was a certain compensation in seeing his two sons escape what he had wanted to escape, and I think he died happy for us and for what we had found in life. Out of all this has come to me an abhorrence for the business world, a hatred of the triumphant industry of our contemporary life, which is perhaps one of the central motives of my life. I find it easy to understand and sympathize with Gandhi in his rebellion against our western industrialism. For I feel that modern capitalism is sapping the lives of millions who were made for better things. I can see all around me men and women who yearn to find in life what life has never brought them. Day after day they toil at the commercial machine, and go home night after night empty of reward and hungry of desire. What wonder that the multitudes today chase madly after any form of entertainment or wild excitement that will give them escape even for a moment from the hell of daily labor. I would wipe out this hell if I could, whatever the consequences, if only for the sake of giving some promise to men of a better world and a happier day. For the minds and souls of men need to be fed as well as their bodies. Something besides money and profits and material goods needs to be chased, and found. My father never had a chance, most men never have a chance, in those matters that pertain to the higher interests of life. I was given my chance, and took it. From that hour on I have felt dedicated to the task of using it for the liberation of those less fortunate than myself.

If there is any one thing which I most like to recall in connection with my father, it is that he grew throughout his life. He was never old, even when his body was broken and his mind dim. He started with little education, and made his own way in the rich treasury of literature and of art. He worked himself free from the entanglements of orthodox Christianity, and followed on and on the adventurous highway of free thought. He was reared in the individualism of the nineteenth century, and in his last years welcomed the Socialism of the twentieth century. He grew up enamoured of all the familiar tradition of war, and died a convicted pacifist. He revered tradition and respected convention, but was always ready for a discovery of new truth and an experiment with new experience. He moved with the changes in the literature, philosophy, science, politics and religion of his time, and never found a stopping-place. From him I derived a momentum of the spirit which has carried me to this day, and which I trust may speed me ever to new goals.

To

VACHEL THOMAS LINDSAY

by

NICHOLAS VACHEL LINDSAY

Springfield, Illinois

Quacks feared him, patent-medicine men feared him, liars feared him with a deadly fear—mothers and sons loved him.

* * * *

The Sermon on the Mount harnessed the savage in the Doctor. The Oath of Hippocrates harnessed the citizen.

NICHOLAS VACHEL LINDSAY

THE DOCTOR

THE Doctor was born near Napoleon, Gallatin County, Kentucky. At the end of the Civil War, he attended Miami Medical College, Cincinnati. He practiced several years in the country region, Cotton Hill, Sangamon County, Illinois. Then he studied abroad a year, specializing in obstetrics in the Vienna hospitals. For the remainder of his life, he was a citizen of Springfield, Illinois, which is not too far from Cotton Hill. The unique thing which is the basis of this tribute, was his loyalty to those farmers who took care of him when he was a boy. He was the doctor in the Cotton Hill region, and this in spite of a very large subsequent practice in Springfield. Every trip over those muddy roads was at a definite loss of money, time, strength, and public prestige of a sort, but he was always grateful to Cotton Hill for taking care of a lonely boy from Kentucky, heartbroken from the Civil War.

THE BROKEN BUGGIES

The Doctor kept two buggies, and nearly always one of them was broken, and being mended. Sometimes both of them were broken. He might drive at midnight on a sudden call over a rutted, frozen, mud road, maybe twenty miles. Quite often, halfway to his destination in the pitch-black night, a deeper rut would twist a wheel or smash a buggy shaft, though the shafts were always reinforced with iron. On those occasions the Doctor would pull out the important medicines and instruments from the back of the buggy, leave all the necessary harness on the horse, leave the rest of it in the buggy, pile the old buffalo robe on the horse, pick up his broken whip, his lantern, his medicine, his instruments, and gallop on through the dark to save mother and child. Next morning he would wake me up, we would go out to that chariot in the ditch with a freshly mended one, and the fresher horse from the stable. We would tie the remains of the broken chariot back of the good chariot, sometimes with a dragging plank supporting where the wheel had been, and the broken buggy would go back into the mending shop and the Doctor would go on with his day's work in town, transferring all medicine and instruments to the fresher chariot.

THE MEDICINE AND INSTRUMENTS

The Doctor was a moving hospital in his equipment of instruments. The buggy was completely stuffed with these, and medicine he mixed himself. He kept to his country doctor habits acquired at Cotton Hill when a doctor had to have a complete drug store and emergency hospital all his own. To the end of his life, the traveling salesmen for the standard drug houses and instrument houses took him in on their regular Springfield rounds. He did not hesitate to give Bitters; his first remedy for sin was castor oil. He could instantly purge away more wickedness than any preacher or any Mussolini, and the meaner they were, the more he gave them something to think about. Often he dispensed with all medicine and used his hereditary Kentucky glare for sinners or blunderers and often took that journey at midnight, bringing into the sick room only the frayed whip.

THE WHIP

The Doctor never used the whip for actual whipping except to encourage a horse he dearly loved, at midnight on a frozen road, but he carried the whip in his hand when he stepped into a farmer's house to give his famous treatment to cure delirium tremens. He did not shake the whip but he carried it. We will suppose a typical case where the farmer for several days had been driving the women and children screaming to the barn and where he was now rolling on the floor seeing reptiles. The Doctor would stand across the room and turn on him eyes that blazed like drills that bore into steel and granite, that burned like Vesuvius. All that he would have to say would be, *"Get up, Jake,"* in a certain tone of voice well known in Kentucky at a crisis involving any kind of whip. Jake would sit up and say, very meekly, "Is that you, Doc?" And the women would bless God. Jake would be cured for at least a year at the expense of one broken buggy, one tired horse, one desperately weary and magnificently furious Doctor and three words said. I recommend the broken buggy and horsewhip treatment to families who are considering giving the patient three years of psychoanalysis and petting. The Doctor could scare the vinegar out of any brute on earth in one minute. He charged two dollars for these treatments and generally took it in cord wood the next spring.

Whatever their complaints or diseases, there was a time when he treated white people for two dollars a call. He always treated Africans for nothing. They loved him well. They knew. They understood. They bowed down their hearts to him.

THE HORSES

Only a Kentuckian will understand when I speak of the Doctor's two Kentucky horses, kept fed and fit and burning, ramping in the stable, almost foundered with good food, and loving him like a Deity. They would arrive at old Cotton Hill through the most fearful sleet, like fire engine horses going to a fire. They were more human than many of the people he pulled through to life and love again. And I fancy, if consulted, the Doctor would have said that many of these were merely midnight adventures with Charley and Tom, the horses. They were brothers of his, staging

Kentucky races, in wicked, reprehensible Republican Illinois, to be saved only by grace.

THE BIBLE

The wild Doctor and the wild horses were terrific foes of woe and weariness. Pioneer blood was in them both and life was always to them a frontier. The Doctor's Bible was more worn than his whip and he would read to the sick. He preferred good hearts, though even the wicked loved him. He read them the Beatitudes, and gave calomel and mercury.

He took out all his passion for fighting, in splendid faithfulness. When I walk in the business section of Springfield, and meet the old retired farmers, I am no one else but the Doctor's son. They proclaim his feats of magic, forty years ago. It is the highest praise any tottering old men can give me in Springfield (and they know it), to call me "the Doctor's son." He helped half the population of Sangamon County safely into the world in his day. The greatest and gentlest obstetrician of his time, and place, it was his record through a long period that he had never lost a mother. Vienna did not teach him in vain. Besides making him gentle, and putting completely into harness passions like those of the red Indian, the Bible kept him a democrat, a desperate believer in the equality of all white men. Just as Cotton Hill left its stamp on him forever. And when he was a very old man, he had the last horse and the last buggy in Springfield. Slick young doctors whose grandmothers he had saved, whose fathers he had helped into the world, looked out from their automobiles in wonder. Why the horse covered with foam and mud? Why the unwashed wheels? Why the buggy that rattled like a threshing machine? Why the funny fifty-year-old buffalo robe dangling to the shafts? Well, the Doctor was a Bible democrat, so he did not lean out of his chariot and say to the brilliant young scientist from Johns Hopkins, "Your father was paid for by two dollars' worth of cord wood in the spring."

The Doctor had another bible besides the Bible. The oath of Hippocrates in very large type, handsomely done, was nailed to the wall of his waiting-room. Therefore the Doctor was expert in ten thousand kinds of silence. He sleeps at old Oak Ridge Cemetery not far from Lincoln's Tomb. Buried with him are the secrets of all in that place, and the Doctor will never tell, and Oak Ridge will never tell. Hippocrates among the immortals has crowned him with bays, for his silence, integrity, and splendor.

I get a thrill when I see in the medical magazines tributes to the old family practitioners. The main points of praise are (1) their all-around knowledge of the complete human being, and (2) their knowledge of definite families, which are fairly balanced against the modern fanatical specialist knowledge. In the roll call of the general practitioners, he will stand near the head, for all those that knew him. Quacks feared him, patent-medicine men feared him, liars feared him with a deadly fear—mothers and sons loved him.

THE OLD MAN IN THE SILK HAT

The Sermon on the Mount harnessed the savage in the Doctor. The oath of Hippocrates harnessed the citizen. My brothers, let me say he was not too much of a democrat. His Kentucky pride was stronger than any medicine he ever gave. That made the whip in his eye. What was he seeing when he did not seem to be attentive? He was haunted by a perpetual vision. This was his old Kentucky father, Nicholas Lindsay, blind, living at the end of the Civil War in an old cabin. The old man had had all his horses stolen by Northern and Southern cavalry, the panicky negroes were stampeded to the ends of the earth, and the largest farm in Gallatin County was taken away by mortgages engineered by the dictators of the district in war time. So the blind old man was given a cabin by his half-grown children, and there he assembled that patriarchal tribe and whipped up their pride to victory. Not one of them failed him in the battle for a place in the world, after the Civil War. The old Southerner was not vanquished even in finery. He carried a gold-headed cane. He wore a long-tailed black coat, and, rain or shine, a stately old-fashioned plug silk hat. My father saw in a vision, all his days, the steel-nerved patriarch striding about, blind, and magnificent with hat and cane, urging his sons to victory, and a victory not of this world.

Just as my father looked back to that proud, imperious and unbroken lord of Kentucky, so do I, his son, look back to him, all his life the terrific foe of woe and weariness. And sometimes *he* too wore a silk hat, on Sunday, in his youth, when he had time to go to church—his splendid and adored young wife, Catharine Frazee Lindsay, walking with great respect beneath the shadow of the cavalier's black plume. I memorialized her in the song:—"The Hearth Eternal," and he is, by metaphor, the "Doctor Mohawk" in the poem of that name, a poem considered so obscure it is not reprinted here. But these two poems give the two sides of my heart.

To

DWIGHT L. MOODY

by

PAUL DWIGHT MOODY

President, Middlebury College

I am deeply grateful that by his wisdom I had to work for a living. . . .

*   *   *   *

The life he lived was greater than any sermon he ever preached. . . .

*   *   *   *

I believe he was the most democratic man in the last century.

PAUL DWIGHT MOODY

NOT the least of my obligation to my father, after the fact of existence itself, is one for which I have always been grateful, a sound body and a good physique. He tried, throughout my boyhood, to secure for me the advantages he had as a boy in living in a simple manner, generally barefooted, always in the country, and to which he in turn owed so much.

I owe him, in addition to this, memories and the influence of a home always happy, comfortable, unshadowed, and singularly blessed in the health of its members; and the picture also of perfect married happiness. His children owe him the privileges of education. Never having himself gone beyond the lowest grades in formal schooling, he was ambitious that we should have the privileges denied him in youth by poverty.

So great is my sense of debt to him that I am only selecting certain items in his credit account. One is a recognition of the dignity of labor, and the realization that any honest toil is worthy. He brought this lesson home to me when I was a boy of fourteen. We were staying together in an institution he had established and which still bears his name. He asked me to black his shoes. The apparatus for this task was in the basement. I put the shoes in a bag and carried them down. On my way back he saw that bag and sensed that I had been ashamed to carry the shoes through the corridor and lobby in my hand. When he had finished talking to me I felt like the meanest, poorest snob, and had I had occasion to repeat the experience I would have carried the shoes at arm's length over my head.

I owe him countless opportunities and openings that have come to me because I am his son. There was a time when, in foolish pride, I felt this almost too heavy a burden and longed to stand on my own feet. I have found that this chance came also.

I am deeply grateful that by his wisdom I have had to work for a living. He received in his time such sums of money that he might have died a wealthy man as the world then reckoned wealth. He died rich, but not in gold, for he gave away what came to him beyond that required for the simple needs of my mother, and this I have never for the briefest second regretted when I have seen what inherited wealth has done to some people I have known. Many have faced the danger well and nobly, but I personally am glad that I have been spared that hard trial.

My deepest gratitude is for what he himself was. Some men, whose lives have been lived in public as much as his was, have neglected their children, and have used up their moral energy in denouncing evil and in private have been peevish, or selfish. In other words, they have not practiced what they preached. The life he lived was greater than any sermon he ever preached, for he was the gentlest and most humble and consistent of men. When my conscience troubled me about boyish offenses, some I must admit seeming slighter in importance now than I felt them then, it was to him more often than to my mother that I confessed them.

One incident must be told because it impressed me deeply then and its impress has never faded. It was when I was, I suppose, in the vicinity of ten years old. He had told me to go to bed. I honestly thought he meant when I had finished a quite legitimate and proper occupation, for I was hobnobbing with a little crony of my age who had come to the house with an older person. I remained talking with him. My father, later passing through the room and finding that I had not obeyed him, spoke with that directness of which he was capable, called brusqueness by some, and ordered me to bed at once. There was no standing on the order of my going after this. I retreated, frightened and in tears, for such a tone of voice was a new experience in my life. I hurried to bed, but before I had time to fall asleep he was at my bedside, kneeling and asking my forgiveness for the harsh way in which he had spoken to me, the tears falling down over his rugged, bearded face.

That was nearly half a century ago, but I would exchange any memory of life before I would surrender that, for all unknowing he was laying for me the consciousness of the Fatherhood of God, and the love of God. No sermon on the prodigal's father, and no words on the love of God have cast quite such a light as his huge figure kneeling in the twilight by my bed, asking the forgiveness of a child. Never since then have I

paused to remember that without a mist in the eyes.
Call it sentimental if you will, it has influenced me
more profoundly than anything else in my life.

My debt to him for the sanity of his faith and his
outlook on life is great. He came out of an age un-
troubled by some of the questions which perplex us.
He was twenty-two when Darwin turned the thinking
world upside down, and ten years older before the
English-speaking branches of the church felt the im-
port of what Colenso was the first to say. He lived to
a day when the edge of these things had penetrated
deeper. It is impossible to say what effect they would
have had upon him had he lived twenty years longer,
or been born twenty years later, two very different
things. But despite the rugged simplicity of his own
creed and his loyalty to his convictions, he was remarkably tolerant of others and in this most unlike a great
many of his professed admirers and followers. Shortly
before he died he remarked that liberal views of the
scriptures, though distasteful to him, had never done
so much harm as savage attacks upon the liberals which
thirty years ago were more common than now. His affection for George Adam Smith and Henry Drummond,
and his admiration for them as preachers, angered
many people, but their anger never worried him. He
was so companionable with certain Roman Catholics
that it was an offense to many. He could not understand them, but he did like them. I believe he was the
most democratic man in the last century, and one with

the broadest sympathies. Some would question this, but they did not know him.

A few years ago I felt compelled to say something of this kind in a religious paper. It called down savage attacks, in which I was called an unworthy son and other names. Fortunately I saw only one of these, shown me by a well-meaning friend. It hurt me more, I presume, than I realized, for the night after seeing this retort to my statement, I had a dream of my father, alive once more and asking me to come with him while he looked at a house in the vicinity where I now live. Knowing his deep attachment to his boyhood home I could not understand why he wanted another house and I asked him why he was locating here. In my dream, with wonderful tenderness in his eyes, such tenderness as I had often seen there, he replied, "Because I want to be near you," and then he kissed me, and in my dream I could feel the contact of his heavy beard as I had so often felt it as a boy. I awoke, with no more sense of hurt at what people had said, for I felt that he understood, as he had always understood.

To

JACOB PICKENS

by

WILLIAM PICKENS

*National Association for the Advancement of
Colored People*

It must have meant something for a little black
American child to grow up without fear, especially
in the South.

*   *   *   *

My father's confidence in me was not deliberate and designing, or it would not have been
effective. . . . He always believed me and believed in me. I cannot remember a single occasion
when he manifested the slightest doubt of my
word or of me.

WILLIAM PICKENS

FATHER would think it a queer discussion, as to what any of us children could "owe" him. He doubtless lived out his nature, acting upon us toward his own greatest satisfaction, as we were parts of him,—parts that sometimes contributed pleasure, sometimes inflicted pain. He lived to near the end of his seventy-fifth year.

There were ten children. Two died before I was born, or before my memory began. I was the sixth child but the first boy. The first boy might be spoiled, but the sixth baby in a large family without luxuries and battling for existence is less likely to be spoiled. Father was the dark-skinned, dark-and-woolly-haired giant who came and went between our little home and the outer world—our sure defender, last authority and ideal of mighty power. One child's father may be a general or a president and another's a store-keeper or a tenant farmer, but the child's mind levels them: each of these men, so differently placed, is to his own child the hero of ultimate reliability. I acknowledge endowments, physical, intellectual and moral or spiritual, from this person whom I knew first as farmer, then as day-laborer and practical mechanic and engineer about a southern city, and finally as a sweet-tempered, loving and lovable old man in his seventies, who smiled amid pains to the end of his life.

The foundation of all other life is physical life. Among all of the ten children of Jacob Pickens, eight of whom I knew well, there was not the slightest deformity of body or mind. All were straight of limb and apparently strong of intellect. Until the question was asked me, I had scarcely reflected on the fact that for thirty-five years, since I was a high-school lad, I have been constantly well; and that through my entire career in school and college, the strength of my body was the admiration of my fellows. When I was past forty-five my friends began to take pleasure, when introducing me to strangers, in raising the question of my years. The great majority guessed me to be at least ten years younger; only one guessed as high as forty years; and several put it as low as twenty-five!

Father was undoubtedly the chief foundation of our physical qualities. Mother was a medium-sized brown woman, whose paternal grandfather was a Cherokee Indian. With bearing and rearing ten children, amid constant work, she used up her life in forty years. Father was reputed to be one of the strong and fearless men of the community in the little South Carolina village where I was a little child. As a henchman of Ben Dacus, the white man who headed one of the rival political factions that dominated the town, he helped to rule the place—by his physical prowess. Dacus as a Confederate soldier had lost four fingers off one hand, leaving only a thumb on that "nubbin." In the political campaigns he used to boast that with this "nubbin" and his one good hand, and with my father's two sound iron fists, the pair of them could "lick" all the leaders of the opposing political faction. They generally made good. And that is how they demonstrated the superiority of their politics and carried most of the elections.

These were formative years, before I reached the age of seven. It must have meant something for a little black American child to grow up in his early years without fear and with a feeling of the capacity for self-defense, especially in the South. Time and time again in the last twenty-five years, observers who have seen me at work in the social struggle of colored people for their rights, and exhibiting what appeared (to them) the courage of unambiguous statements and uncompromising claims, have remarked: "Your spirit and naïve fearlessness are a puzzle to us, *when we reflect that you were born and raised in the South.*" Children learn "panicky" fear early or maybe not at all. In all of my life I have never once been conscious of an unnerving fear of anything or anybody. Twice has my destruction been definitely planned by mobs, and on two other occasions in the South I have been threatened with immediate death by shooting, at one time the gun being actually drawn and coming to aim. I think it was expected that I would run or quail. I did not, and something seemed to come into the arm of the gunman, causing him to drop his weapon back into his pocket. I was at that time sixteen years of age, while my father was still a mighty man at forty-seven. Afterwards the gunman, an officer and a known killer, coolly remarked: "I would have killed you, if I hadn't thought of your father." And perhaps it was not only the respectability and good citizenship of my father that flashed through his head.

All of this does not mean that I failed in any way, or in any case, to *realize the danger*. But one may realize ultimate danger, may take every step to avert it, may even despair of avoiding it, without being afraid. Twice at least, thoroughly conscious of the chances against me, I have fully considered myself lost, so far as life is concerned,—looking right at the end of it and counting its remainder in minutes. And I resolved to use all human means against the threatened evil, but that was all. I know of no foundation for this, unless it be that the courage, strength and devotion of our father saved us, since we were tiny tots, from having to reckon with fear. Certainly our mother, while having the patience and long-suffering known only to burdened housewives, had also in the face of any extraordinary danger the usual timidity of women who are unlettered and very religious or a bit superstitious.

Jacob Pickens was not a man of heroic physical proportions. I am five feet ten inches, and he was at least two inches shorter. When I remarked to him that my son is at least six feet, or two inches taller than I am, father informed me that he was also a bit taller than his father, and that the generations must be "rising." From my slave grandfather to my son is a regular ascending stairway. Physical development, at least, is very much dependent upon environment. But father was stockily built, with muscles hardened by continual work, and a patience to endure hardships of every kind. His temper was respected, rising rapidly, but he was never deliberately cruel. Such a man does not lack the respect of his neighbors. Often he excelled in rustic contests: corn-huskings, wood-choppings, tree-fellings and "log-rollings." When the logs of the felled and trimmed trees were to be removed from the land that was being cleared, the neighbors from miles around would gather to see who was "the best man," with the mightiest muscles and the most unbreakable back. On such occasions many a contest of utter strength would be staged, called a "log-rolling": two men would take positions, one on either side of some giant log, and with their poles under it as prying implements, each would do his best to roll it against the other. One still wonders why a people, with too much hard and grilling work upon them most of the time, would make their "play" by staging contests of the most dangerous and back-breaking rivalry. The performance of our western "lumber jacks," spinning a log in the water under their feet without losing their balance, requires skill and control, but nothing like the sheer muscle-might of those "log-rollings" of the Negro farmers, sometimes with one man on each side of the log, and sometimes with two or more contestants on each side. In all of such feats of primitive strength father was a frequent winner and the admiration of his fellow rustics—and naturally the hero of his family. Saying that his "hand was too heavy," he was accustomed to leave the management, correction and chastisement of the children to

our mother; so that he seldom used "the rod," but
when he did, it was an event. Our mother died when I
was but thirteen years of age, and there were three children younger than I; but after her death I do not recall
that he ever resorted to corporal punishment for any
of his children.

I do not use alcoholic drinks or tobacco—and there
is not the slightest grain of either religion or "morals"
in the fact. I know how it happened. Physical manli-
ness is about the first thing of the kind a boy may admire. I admired father's physical excellence, and he was
not a smoker. I did not therefore associate smoking
with "being a man"—but quite the opposite. And when
at school and at about the age when boys will take to
tobacco we reached the lessons in physiology, I read
that tobacco was bad for the child: that it weakened
the heart, stunted the growth, lessened the strength.
Whether that be true or false, it was sufficient for me
at this period, when I was being sorely tempted to go
along with the other boys and smoke behind the teacher's back, for the exquisite pleasure of violating a rule
that was dictated without reasons or proofs. But the
book gave a reason: weakness. That was different.
Father was strong.—But how about alcohol? Father
used "strong drink," and even did some boasting about
how much he could take down and never get drunk,
while those who were vying with him would be "knocked
out" on much less. And ever since I can remember, I
had heard of corn-whiskey, gin, rock-and-rye, brandy,
wines, and later on of beers. They used to take water

and sugar and season it with a bit of liquor, calling the
mixture a "toddy," and give it to us children early
mornings, to start us right and keep us healthy. I had
also read in the school books that alcohol was bad for
boys. But father was a standing contradiction to that,
for he used whiskies and was never drunk or otherwise
mastered by drink. Perhaps it was bad for weak boys.
But one day the bottle of white whiskey hidden under
the bed was discovered by two of us children, the sister
next to me in age and myself. "Straight whiskey" had
never been for us, and naturally we wanted to try our
hands, or rather our stomachs, on the real and unadul-
terated. The stuff was so fiery that we could but touch
our tongues to it, but courageously we kept at it, returning every little while to draw the cork and brave
the mighty liquid. I do not remember how often we did
that, nor do I recall anything else for the remainder
of that day.—But next morning when I waked up, my
older sisters and a young aunt were having the fun of
their lives telling and laughing over the events of the
day before: I learned from their hilarious conversation
that my last act on the day before was an effort to step
from the top to the bottom of the stairs in one single
stride. Although I was not injured in bone or muscle, I
was evidently "out." But from that day, forty years
ago, until the present moment, I have not taken a
drink of alcoholic liquor of any sort. Was it because
these laughing girls shamed me, or even tried or meant
to shame me? Not at all. Their banter was of the
most good-natured kind: I was the pet of the family

that day. They thought it the best of fun. Their challenge was of the sort that would have made the average boy go to it again, to show them: for they were simply amused because the stuff had downed me, and that I was not quite strong enough for it—yet. But the word of my father turned the tables—and a word it was, void of either reprimand or command—a simple comment without either smile or frown. And the words were addressed, not to me individually, but to the high-larking company as a whole. The exact words I cannot recall, but the tenor of them was this: "Of course the liquor had knocked the boy out. It is neither a sign of weakness nor of strength to be unable to stand liquor; whiskey, like some other things, is very bad and ruinous to some people. But it would be a cowardly weakness to know that it is bad for you and then to take it. My little son had never known before that it was bad for him, but he knows it now as well as any one else."—That really settled it: the stuff was not good for me, and my strength lay in the ability to chuck it aside. What neither precept nor command nor ill-grounded "moral suasion" may accomplish, may be induced by ambition and emulation.—On many occasions since that day many jolly friends in many parts of the world have tried in vain to get me to take a simple drink of some alcoholic beverage or other: "Come on! Just a sip! It won't hurt you, it's good for you." I have never felt the slightest temptation and therefore no virtue or righteousness in my refusal. I have sometimes felt a slight embarrassment at the evi-

dent embarrassment of some sensitive friend to whom
there was no opportunity to explain that there was
neither religion nor politics in my attitude. I never feel
the slightest inclination to prevent anybody else from
drinking or smoking. It was just a child's resolve of
long, long ago, concerning himself and with no refer-
ence to others.

The eight of father's children, whom I knew well,
seemed normal in mind, as in body. Two had phe-
nomenal memories and always headed their classes, so
long as they could stay in school. But practically all of
them dropped out early, as the children of the poor
must do.

Acquaintances of mine have often remarked how
easily I seem to get on with people younger than myself, with mere children in fact. It is a characteristic
also noticeable in all of my three children: that even as
large youths, they could still enjoy the companionship
of very little tots. Their grandfather had a magnetism
for the young until the day of his death. If he came
into a new community, within a very short while most
of the tots and youngsters and youths would be calling
out to him as he passed by. This love for little children
developed by suggestion in all of his children a regard
for the young and a sympathy for the weaker. I never
saw one of my brothers or sisters doing what in the
fraternity of our house was always accounted the most
cowardly of crimes: imposing on a smaller or a weaker
person. On Sunday mornings he used to lead his tots to
the Sunday school. He and mother had taught them-

selves to read in their youth, after they were married, but never to write well. The church was the one center of culture, and in the Sunday school he could indulge, with others, in mental gymnastics about Jonah and his whale, Balaam and his ass, Daniel and his lions, and such other indeterminable subjects of discussion.

But there is one disposition of soul, or habit of mind, which my father, unconsciously perhaps, helped to influence in me, and which is for me the greatest hindrance or help—I do not know which. I will try to describe, and to indicate how I think it was developed if not created.—A few years ago the Negro women of America bought and dedicated as a national shrine on Anacostia Heights, Washington, D. C., the home of Frederick Douglass, who was by all measurements the greatest ex-slave that the western world has produced. At the dedication exercises it was my task to deliver an address on the life of Frederick Douglass and its meaning. When I was returning from the Heights, Mrs. Mary Church Terrell, internationally known colored woman leader, walked by my side, and as we abandoned the echoes and scenes of the historic occasion, she said: "I think I discovered today why, when you speak, we believe what you say and are influenced by it: it is because you seem to believe it yourself." My reply to her intended compliment was equally sincere: "And I *seem* to believe it because I *believe* it."—Many of those who read this, may recall how they have said to me the same thing, perhaps in other words: "Your ring of utter sincerity influences us." Hundreds of times southern white persons have come forward out of the audience: "We did not come out expecting to agree with you, but we like the way you put your case." Sometimes those whose prejudices and ideas had evidently been contradicted, have said simply: "It is good that we have heard the *other side*."

How did a plain American Negro father, unschooled and unknown to the public platform, and therefore without any wish or design so to do, happen to influence the development of this disposition? For even after nearly a half century of life I still believe that if the truth be spoken simply, bravely and without too many artificial decorations, even those who do not like you, must believe it and receive it. My better acquaintance with the people of the world has shown me, several times, that selfish and designing lies, reenforced by flattery, may become dangerous rivals against plain, unflattering truth.—But what had father to do with this reputed disposition to believe earnestly and to speak convincingly? Simply this: that he always believed me and believed in me. I cannot remember a single occasion when he manifested the slightest doubt of my word or of me. When I was a very little child, I was doubtless sometimes led to conceal or to deny the truth to dodge a whipping, because of the strange notion of grown-ups that the truth should be punished; but such incidents are not now within the reaches of my memory. But since the beginning of my clear memory there was no doubt whatever that my father would have believed my

word under any circumstances. Therefore I never had
to hesitate, for fear of not being believed by the person who mattered most after my mother had died. Even
before that time, when I was eight years old and we
lived on an Arkansas farm, I once played a trick on
somebody, which turned out to be a very vexing trick
on my father. As I wandered through the melon patch,
I accidentally stumbled upon a large fine watermelon
that was carefully concealed by having the long grass
blades drawn over it. It was evident that somebody
was reserving this particular melon. As a mean joke
on this somebody, I carefully turned the melon over,
without severing it from the vine, cut a good large
square out of its under side, removed and ate all the
"heart," then packed it full of dirt, replaced the square
of the rind and turned it right-side-up again. For days
I waited to see who should pluck and cut this sand-
hearted melon. It proved to be father, who had reserved
it for guests on some occasion. When he cut it and discovered the "ornery" trick, he was furious, and he
made a mistake: he threatened what he would do to the
one who had played the trick. Then he began to inquire, and when he looked in my direction (as the gods
would have it!) he stopped the inquiry. At that time it
seemed that I was saved by a miracle; but in later years
I reasoned that he could clearly "see" who was guilty,
and repented himself of his hasty threats. Perhaps he
instinctively avoided forcing me to deny it,—for that
was going to be one of the best opportunities, and to
me one of the most justifiable occasions for stout lying

that I have ever met with in all my life. The subject never came up again for nearly thirty-five years, and then we could laugh about it.

On the other hand, this experience of being believed has caused me to appear to others, sometimes, as disagreeably frank. It has incapacitated me for fine flattery. An uncompromising position and an unambiguous statement of it are of the essence of my life. And I believe that it is not the quality of my will but the habit of my nerves; not character but characteristic. Not that I would have any more moral scruples against lying my way to success, than have many other men; but in that I would have no skill. Frankness and straightforwardness are the only strength of my going. For a cause and to comrades in whom I did not believe, I would be a clumsy liar and a most unhappy flatterer. I am conscious of a powerful reaction when some one seems to doubt my word, in a business transaction or from the platform. My greatest inspiration in making a speech is when there is an opposing speaker, or opposition in the minds of the audience. It is like an athlete who expects to win but feels the presence of a more formidable opponent. I reflect now on the audacity with which I entered all contests from the public schools through Yale College: I always expected to win, never had the slightest idea of losing. At Yale I entered an oratorical contest, and I gave up the job I had for earning my board, in order to devote more time to the contest, because the money to be received by the winner of the first prize would pay my board for the rest of the year! When the reporter in Little Rock, Arkansas, looked up my father to tell him the news and to get some expression from him, they say that the reporter wavered between amusement and vexation at the naïve response: "Yes, I knew Willie was going to win."—My father's confidence in me was not deliberate and designing or it would not have been effective. It was real, simple. I can see him now, when I was a sixteen-year-old high school lad and was about to start a boat race across the Arkansas River, single-handed in my boat but against two grown men in the other boat: he is coolly offering to bet any bystander that I will win. When the race was over, he boasted unhesitatingly: "Of course he won—that's my blood!" He had no money with which to help me, but he also seemed to have no *doubt* that I could make my way through high school and college. The danger of his apparently unlimited confidence in me was perhaps counteracted by the difficulties which I met in having to battle my own way along,—and by the abundant indifference of many others and the keen opposition of a few.

When father was seventy years old, he remarked reflectively that in all of my life I had never given him one hour of trouble. That, I think, only meant that he had never been able to misdoubt or to blame me, whatever happened. For when I was a high school lad, we were all celebrating on the Fourth of July the opening of the first "free bridge" over the Arkansas River at Little Rock. As I mingled with the merry-makers in North Little Rock, I came upon a gang of eight or ten

white boys who tried to force me off the sidewalk into
the gutter. I was working that summer vacation in the
"stave factory," and was as stout and supple as any
young bull. I resolved not to get off into the gutter.
With my back to one of the posts that supported the
shed over the street in front of a store, I was defying
the attack. The gang hesitated and began quibbling
about which one should lead the attack. Then I had an
enlightening experience with a certain type of race
prejudice: The store-keeper had been looking on, with
an inciting grin, from the very beginning of the affair;
but when the gang wavered in its attack, this store-
proprietor yelled for a policeman. Was he summoning
the officer to protect me, because I was being attacked
and was one against eight or ten? I noticed that none
of the boys ran away, and when the policeman arrived
and gruffed out: "Whatsamatter here?" the store-
keeper pointed an accusing finger at me, saying: "Why,
it's that nigger boy—he's goin' to fight all of these
white boys!" I was so astonished that I uttered not a
word, simply obeying the policeman's "Come along
you!" as we started across the river toward the city
jail. When we got to the middle of the bridge, the officer
seemed to notice my silence—perhaps he also noticed
that I was not afraid. He said, "Stop a minute!" and
asked me some questions: where I lived, what was my
name, who was my "folks." As I answered his questions, the ridiculousness of the situation seemed to
dawn upon him, and he said: "Well, you just go on.
They won't know whether you were locked up or not.

Don't say anything about it." That was my first, and to this day my last, unfriendly experience with a policeman.

Meanwhile some of those we met on the bridge knew me, and ran to tell my father that a policeman had me and was on the way to the "calaboose." Father had not waited to go to the bridge—his house was near the river—but had seized a small boat and rowed himself across and rushed to the city jail. He was in such a state of mind that even policemen at headquarters sympathized with him: they told him that I was not there, that my name was not on the docket, that no one had brought me in. But to satisfy him they had to lead him through the entire jail and let him look into all the cells. When he came back home and found me, he said not a word to imply that I could have done anything wrong, simply asking how in the world a policeman had ever made such a mistake as to arrest me, and how the mistake was finally rectified. I told the story. And in spite of the menace which such a situation might bear for him and for me, he said that I was right to stand and fight, rather than to be imposed upon or to run away. Strange, perhaps, but his unconditional faith made me more prudent, to preserve that faith.

To

THEODORE ROOSEVELT

by

THEODORE ROOSEVELT, JR.

Porto Rico

Even when Father was President and over-whelmed with work, both he and Mother made a practice of breakfasting with us. . . .

* * * *

A confidence from a child was just as carefully kept by Father as a confidence from a President. . . .

* * * *

When Father was dressing for dinner we used to gather in his room and he amused us by reciting to us.

THEODORE ROOSEVELT, JR.

To understand a family it is necessary to know what their house is like, for the home where a family grows up is always a part of the background of life for every child. The beauty of the house makes surprisingly little difference to the children. It is what happens there that counts.

"Sagamore" is the offspring of the years as surely as is a reef of coral. Wings and rooms, pictures and furniture. Each tells a story in the same fashion as the rings in the trunk of a great tree. By far the handsomest part of the house is the North Room. It is as large as all the other rooms on the ground floor put together. Father had it built when he was President. Every bit of wood or piece of stone which went into its construction came from the United States or her possessions.

The North Room to me always means evening, a great fire blazing on the hearth, its flickering light dancing on the flags in the gloom of the ceiling, Father, a book under one arm, poking it with a long iron trident, Mother sitting sewing in a corner of the sofa by a lamp.

One of the greatest institutions of the civilized world is the family dining table. Food is not all that can be got from it. When guests were with us there was no ban on the conversation of any one, no matter how small either the individual or the conversation might be, unless the child showed monopolistic tendencies.

Father hated large centerpieces. He used to maintain that he married Mother because he liked to look at her, and did not see why at table she should be concealed behind a mass of foliage. Once he confided to my wife, "Eleanor, these large table decorations are ridiculous. If we go on a picnic we do not select a bush and then sit around it in a circle to have lunch!"

Even when Father was President and overwhelmed with work, both he and Mother made a practice of breakfasting with us. This meant an earlier hour for them than would otherwise have been necessary for we had to go to school. In both generations the table has been treated as a gathering place for the family. There has never been a question of the children being served separately in the nursery.

When I had measles Father was Civil Service Commissioner. We were living in a small red-brick house in Washington. There was no room to spare, so in order to isolate me they moved me to Father's dressing room. It was separated only by the thinnest kind of a door from the room where Mother and Father slept. Senator Lodge gave me a small hand organ. It was a joy to me and a torment to the rest of the household. I went to sleep at seven-thirty and woke at five-thirty. Father and Mother went to sleep at twelve and would have liked to wake at eight. As soon as the first daylight found its way through the chinks of the blinds I would grasp my beloved organ and start playing it. It speaks volumes for their forbearance that it was a number of days before I was told that no concerts could be given until after breakfast.

My turn towards natural history was fostered by Father who was a really distinguished amateur scientist. This bent of his developed early. When young, he and a cousin had a museum, which they called the Roosevelt Museum. Out of it grew a really fine collection of birds and small mammals.

Of the many small funerals that stand out in my memory the clearest is that of our dog Jack. He was first buried behind the White House. When Father left the Presidency Mother did not want Jack to stay there, beneath the eyes of Presidents who might care nothing for little black dogs. His coffin was dug up and he was brought to Oyster Bay. One summer afternoon we had the second interment. The hearse was a wheelbarrow. We boys, Mother and Father were the pallbearers and mourners. Solemnly we walked across the lawn. Then the comedy of the double funeral struck Father. With difficulty he stifled his laughter, for fear of hurting Mother's feelings. Almost choking with the effort he glanced at Mother, and saw that what he thought was grief smothered in a handkerchief was really laughter. She as well as he had been overcome by the comic side of six full-grown people conducting a second funeral for a dog with the aid of a wheelbarrow.

One of the most delightful of our outdoor recreations during the summer was camping. This consisted of the

male parent taking the male children to spend the night
on some beach or in some wood near Oyster Bay.

When we were little Father took us all camping in
this fashion. Now my brothers and I in our turn do the
same with our children. Needless to say the point of
view on the trip is entirely different when you are ten
and conducted and when you are forty and conduct.
To the boy of ten it is an odyssey of adventure, where
anything may happen from the advent of strange unknown wild animals to combats with outlaws. To the
disillusioned grown-up of forty the happenings are all
too well known.

Father was pilot, cook, raconteur, and disciplinarian.
I never realized the extent of his good temper until it
came my turn to take my children in similar fashion.
It did not occur to me in those days that he could do
other than enjoy being dirty with a good excuse. I can
see him now in the misty gray of a rainy morning pad-
dling down a shell-strewn beach in his bare feet, a
toothbrush in his hand, to where the water swished
oilily around the reed-clothed rocks.

Mother once described to me an Easter at Albany
during Father's term as Governor. Both of them were
hiding the presents. It was late at night and Father
was tired after a long hard day's work. He put one
present on the gas globe, where it was in plain sight.
Mother protested, saying that any one could see it
there. Father defended himself and explained that the
principle always advanced in detective stories was that

the obvious was never evident. He was right. That was the last present found.

Of course we went to church. I have been in many great cathedrals which "set tall towers against the dawn," where the music rolled sonorously through the vaulted naves whose wealth of detail melted into darkness, but to me, church always means the little chapel at Oyster Bay where we went as children and where my children in turn attended.

Next to our church stood the modest parish house where Sunday school was held. When we were old enough we were encouraged by Father and Mother to teach.

We always try to do unto a child as we would be done by. That was Father's policy also. Indeed he observed it so strictly that when we were young we sometimes took advantage of it. A confidence from a child was just as carefully kept by Father as a confidence from a President.

Once when six and eight respectively, Kermit and I were going on an exploring trip. The territory to be traversed was the second and third stories of our house in the country. Like all good explorers we decided we should have caches of food for this dangerous expedition. With a good deal of difficulty we collected from the pantry and kitchen an assortment of supplies—a few prunes, some maple sugar and candy, a few cookies and some crackers. The next step was to find a hiding place. After much debate we decided to put them under the pillow in the spare room bed.

When we had done this we took counsel and decided that if we were found out there would be trouble—even Mother was not broad-minded enough to allow food to be kept in the spare room bed. At once we went to Father and under promise of secrecy told him all about it. That put him on his honor. We finished our expedition and embarked on some other enterprise. The question of the cache slipped from our minds.

A guest came to stay. Our hoard was discovered. In a moment, in the "twinkling of an eye," we were called to the bar of justice. When charged with the crime we made no attempt to deny it, but shrilly protested that Father had known of it all along, thereby "averting the whip of calamity" from our heads and diverting it to him.

When men and women are properly educated the homely, every-day incidents are always correlating themselves with memories of other happenings heard in conversations or read in books. My Father's education was just of this sort. He was one of the most widely read men I have ever known. His knowledge stretched from babies to the post-Alexandrian kingdoms, and what was more, he could always lay his hands on it. He knew the species of Hannibal's elephants through the shape of their ears as shown on the Carthaginian coins of that period. He could recite "The Song of Roland" in the original French. He knew the latest laws adopted in the reorganization of the State government in Illinois. He could tell you in detail the history of the heavyweight boxing champions. It was never safe to contradict him on any statement, no matter how recent you might feel your information was.

When Father read to us we all interrupted him continually with questions, but Kermit was by far the worst offender. One "why" bred another so quickly in his mind that soon the reading almost stopped. Father hit on a device to save the situation. He said he would answer all questions, but "not until the reading was finished for the day." This served a double purpose. It allowed him to read without interruptions and cut down the number of questions greatly, because we forgot all but the last couple. Kermit tried to overcome this difficulty by getting pencil and paper and writing them down as they occurred. In those days his ability as a chirographer was much that of Bill the Lizard. If he wrote carefully it took too long. If he did not, he could not read what he had written. As a result even this device failed.

My father always lived the scenes he recounted and told of small incidents in historic scenes as if he had been there himself. Much of the groundwork of my history I got when as a little boy of eight or nine I walked with him to his office in the morning. As he strode over the wide, tree-shaded, half-empty streets of Washington, I pattered at his side and listened enthralled to tales of "sea fights and land fights grim and great." Occasionally, we would stop and he would draw me in the dust of the gutter the plan of some battle.

Poetry is an endless source of enjoyment to those who are fond of it. There is no reason why all should not be fond of it. If the father and mother will read verses aloud to the children they soon begin to care for it. My first acquaintance with poetry came long before I could read. There were whole poems that I knew by heart just from hearing them repeated by Father and Mother. When Father was dressing for dinner we used to gather in his room and he amused us by reciting to us. In this way I learnt nearly all of "The Rhyme of the Three Sealers" and a dozen other poems.

Since those days I have turned to poetry for pleasure and consolation at many times and in many places. When Kermit and I were traveling in Central Asia, the verse that we had been taught to love stood us in good stead. As we rode mile after mile over the sandy, limitless deserts or through the winding mountain defiles, we recited. Sometimes we would recite antiphonally, sometimes we both would chant the poems together.

To

HENRY VILLARD

by

OSWALD GARRISON VILLARD

The Nation

Citizen of two lands, no narrow nationalism could be his. He abhorred those who seek by metes and bounds to stake out for their selfish selves a part of the world to have it all their own, letting the devil take care of the rest. . . .

* * * *

He hated no man for his color, and feared none because his was a different hue, a different tongue, another faith, a strange and baffling mode of life.

A TRUE FAIRY TALE

by

OSWALD GARRISON VILLARD

I

ONCE upon a time it so befell that in a distant kingdom
there lived a boy thirteen years of age. Now the king
of this country and his ministers ruled his subjects
with an iron hand, they having old-fashioned ideas.
According to these the king declared that he alone was
fit to rule, that he governed because God had chosen
him to do so, and that his subjects should have no
voice in their own ruling, not even that which men call
a Parliament to hear their needs. Now in those days,
as today, there were hot heads to declare that all was
not well in the world, that they were unhappy, that they
wished to sit with the king, and to counsel with him.
Soon they began to murmur threats against his most
gracious majesty, whose loyal vassals declared that he
was both holy and "salved of God." So the day came
when in that part of the kingdom in which the boy
lived (far from the court in which the king dwelt with
his favorites, his courtiers, and his jesters) these mal-
contents rose to declare that the king was king no more
and that they ruled in his stead. And when their names

147

were read out in the market-place, lo, it appeared that this boy's uncle, Fritz, led all the rest.

Now the truth is that the next day was Monday and therefore a day for school. So the little boy put his knapsack with his books upon his back, the sandwich which he ate at noon he bestowed in his pocket, and so he sallied forth. And when it occurred that the class had met the teacher said to him: "Now, do you lead the class today in prayer for our beloved and salved Majesty, the King, even as is done on every day."

But the little boy replied: "Nay, I shall not pray for his salved Majesty, the King, since now there is no King, for it is my uncle who rules in his stead." At this the teacher was aghast, saying: "This is rebellion and a crime. Thou art a traitor. I declare this school adjourned." So the little boy and the other boys went home, but not to play, for none were of the mood to play. The next evening they stood upon the hills and watched. Soon there were what looked like fireflies upon the meadows below. But old men said: "No, these are the flashes of the shots which men fire that they may kill their fellow-men." And when the flashes ceased the old men were troubled and sad, and, with the boys around them, went to their homes.

For it was his salved majesty who had won and the little boy's Uncle Fritz who had lost, for such was then the way of this unhappy world. And when the little boy thereafter asked: "Where is my Uncle Fritz?" his father and mother were downcast and said to him: "Ask not, and know not either." But the day came when their

faces were cheerful and he asked again and they said:
"Know that thy Uncle Fritz is safe in a land far across
the seas and far beyond the sea in a place where live
the Indians that men call Illinois, for there land is free
and men, too, and there is no king and men have say as
to how they shall be ruled." And the little boy said:
"There, too, shall I go some day for I will never pray
for his majesty our king, but for our rightful ruler—
my Uncle Fritz." And the king's rulers in the town
heard of this and said to the boy and his father: "Never
shall this little boy set foot in the school in this town,
for he will not pray for his and our majesty the king."
Thereat the father was sorely troubled and sat for long
in thought. Then he said: "Go hence for a twelvemonth
into exile in a land where men call themselves the
French. There shalt thou go to school, and learn in the
tongue in which they speak. Then shalt thou return to
this, our land, to the home of thy grandsire who lives
some leagues away and there shalt thou learn again,
for there men know not that thou wilt not pray for his
majesty our king."

So the little boy put his knapsack again upon his
back and, setting forth into the world, came ere long
to where lived the men called French, and a year thereafter to where his grandsire lived, in a famous town
under a tall and noble church. But to the home where
dwelt his father and his mother his feet ne'er returned
again save briefly. From the home of his grandsire he
went to school, while he grew and grew as straight and
as tall as a young pine, until one day he, too, took ship

across the seas and landed upon the distant shore. From there the way was long and hard and often the boy's heart all but failed and he thought: "Why did I not stay at home and pray for his majesty the king?" But his heart persevered. After twelve long moons he came unto the land of the Illinois and there found he his Uncle Fritz who cried: "Welcome! Welcome! Come to us, for you were the little boy who at thirteen would not pray for his majesty the king!"

II

The fairies that watched over this boy's cradle were many and they were generous with the gifts they bestowed by the touch of their wands. One made him to be not only tall but strong and handsome, so that when he had grown to manhood men and women looked upon his presence and then at one another, declaring: "He is meant to lead us." Another gave him the desire for adventure and to build new paths through the deserts, the prairies, and the forests primeval. So it once came to pass that leaving the land of the Illinois, he wandered far, far across the plains and into mountains where his own people were few and far between, but where of Indians that the white men feared and of the animals called buffaloes there were many. For some had told that here was to be found a precious substance, called gold, which wiseacres have held to be the root of all evil. Now there were few to believe that there was gold in the Colorados, most opining "Dame Rumor makes

sport of us." Then this youth, having joined two others
of good repute, toiled far into the great hills to see
where adventurers washed the streams and found much
gold, so that they might send back the news for all to
read and believe. And men did, and soon, when the
snows of the winter had passed, there appeared a multitude who had read what the youth and the two others
had written. Later there came the day—but that shall
be told in its place.

Then this youth returned to the land of the Illinois,
caring not to fill his pockets with the gold of the
streams. For another fairy had touched him with her
wand to place within him the desire to express himself
with what is called the pen. This is held to be in some
respects a baleful gift since, if one does not take heed,
it is likely to master him that possesses it. Like some
sicknesses of the blood, there are those to say, once
the itch to write is in a man's veins it is never to be
cast out. So with this youth it was not gold which was
the lure, but the pen to write what he saw and heard,
even in the language that to him was new and strange.
And in the land of the Illinois and elsewhere in that
year, this people who were without a king and ruled
themselves, were torn with dissensions as to what was
right and what was wrong, and whether all men should
be free and equal, or none but those whose skins were
fair. And soon two champions stood forth in Illinois,
one saying that a house divided against itself must fall;
the other that things had better be much as they were.
And they said to one another: "Let us go before our

people at certain times and places, and let us there discuss in the open, under the sky, that those among whom we dwell shall hear and decide which of us tells the truth." Thereupon multitudes came to hear these champions, of whom one was named Lincoln, the Rail-Splitter, while the other men dubbed Douglas, the Little Giant; and in the crowds stood the youth in whose veins was the itch to write, and he wrote what he heard that still other multitudes, who could not come to hear, might chance to read, far, far away.

Now still another fairy had given this man-child courage, steeling him against fear. Soon there came a time when the dissension in this people grew so great that no longer would neighbor discuss with neighbor under the blue sky in quiet and in calm, but, their evil passions gaining control of them, brothers slew brothers, some doing so in order that all might be free and equal, even those of darker skin. So this youth, whom men now called Henry Villard, for four years stood where the flashes of guns, such as he had first seen that evening from the hill-top in his far-off native town, were thickest, writing of the death and life of which he was a part. This was so that the country which had bade him welcome, and made him free to live and learn and prosper, might know what was the dire thing called war, and how bravely its sons fought and died. And those whose duty it was to fight and die looked upon this youth and, seeing that he knew not fear, said: "Behold, he is one of us and we are grateful for what he writes, that our loved ones may hear of us, and what it is that we endure, and how we die."

At last the day arrived when peace was once more in the land, and those who were of dark skins were slaves no more, and it was said that all men were free and equal at last. Then the scribe who had seen these things come to pass, continuing to write that he might have to eat, travelled back across the seas to where there still ruled over his vassals the king that was salved. And with him travelled one who had given her life to him, to have and to hold, which he honored and enriched, even as she his, for some thirty-four years. In time it befell that he, being poor, as happens most often to a scribe, became ill in the land of his fathers, and there as he rested to become well again, men waited on him asking: "Give us thy aid. Thou knowest this land called America and the tongue which there men speak; thou hast been across the plains and into the mountains of the Colorado and hast seen the laying of the iron rails upon which people now travel across the wastes. To some that have laid these rails we gave of our treasure for a large return. No longer do we receive the return and are we now afraid for our treasure. Do thou go back across the seas and save the sums that are ours." And the scribe, heeding their call for aid, now being well again, laid aside his pen for all time and departed on their behalf.

So this scribe was scribe no more, but became what is known as a man of large affairs and, because still another fairy had touched him with her wand, he became rich and powerful beyond his fairest hopes. Thus it happened that he pioneered again, blazing new paths through the endless plains and the forests primeval. Soon built he ships that moved by steam, and himself laid the rails that were also sought that those who wished might enter promised lands. For wherever he went this man saw where others were blind. Where there were deserts he beheld the farms and the homes to come and the crops that were to flower where none had ever grown before. Where the rivers descended in falls, there he visioned the mills and the forges to arise and the cities to be. "See," said he; "behold these boundless plains. Upon them shall grow the crops to feed nations far across the globe. Where their people are poor today and cannot buy the grain they need, ours shall come to them for less." And it happened even as he said, for it was bestowed upon him not only to dream dreams, but to dream dreams that came true.

Moreover, it was given to him to win those with whom he talked, so that they came to him with their monies declaring: "This is ours; do thou, Henry Villard, do with it what thou wilt; we ask no bond, but only thy word." For of such was their confidence in him. Then taking their sums, again he laid rails where none had been before, until one day the steel path from East to West, through a trackless empire, was done. Then rose up men to call him great and blessed. "Behold," they cried, "it is a kingdom which he has opened for us with all the treasures of lake and stream and of mountains wherein are gold and silver and copper and iron to make fortunes for us all." Thereupon when he, who had been but a foreign boy without means at all, and a poor unknown scribe writing in words that were not native to his tongue, travelled the first over this new path of steel, it was in conveyances beflagged and festooned, to drive the last of all the many million spikes that held down the rails. It was as if a beloved king were travelling through his land, for men and women and children thronged to see and cheer him who had completed what others had sought in vain to do, making a great nation whole.

III

Now in most all fairy tales it is at this point writ: "And he lived happily ever afterwards, reaping the full reward of his bravery, his fortitude, his virtue, and his unselfishness." But of this fairy tale it was declared at the start that it was true. Hence is the ending otherwise. For not his fortitude, nor his virtue, nor his desire to serve others kept this man in that seat of the mighty to which he had aspired and which he had won. There passed but weeks ere it came to him to learn one of the oldest lessons in the world, that he who falls from on high falls deep and falls hard; that the most of those who applaud success are as quick to denounce those that fail. Riches and power now passed from him; there were those in plenty who sought to tarnish the honor and good name of him upon whom but yesterday they had fawned, seeking the smallest favors at his hands. The shouting and the tumult were indeed o'er. There were few so poor to do him justice. But not for very long. Once more there was a day when men turned to him saying: "He shall lead us again. It was he who saw visions and dreamed dreams, and told of the future like none other. Him let us call once more." So once more came he to the seat of power, even that which he had held before. But it was not as it had been before; there were no new paths to blaze, no new fastnesses to conquer, no more great new States to tie together by bonds of steel; nor did the cheers of the multitude sound as real or as true as in the days before. It was even with him as with the burnt child which dreads the fire. Then, too, adversity was never far beyond the door like the knowledge of the easy faithlessness of many of those one sought to serve. So the time came again when, willingly now, he quitted the seat of might, saying: "Now have I done my best. Let me depart in peace." And then, but not until then, did he live happily afterward among those who loved him truly, in the years that were still bestowed upon him. And so endeth, in this soberwise, this true and honest tale.

IV

To a son, also a scribe, has it fallen to write of this man and of these things; and out of a full and grateful heart has he done so. For he was witness of this man's rise; he beheld the triumphal journey, the last spike. It was given to him as to but few others to know Henry

Villard's modesty in extraordinary success and fortitude in adversity; to understand how little his desire
for personal gain, how great his wish to achieve the
visions which were his. By ambition, we know, fell the
angels; this man faced partial defeat not through ambition, but because he looked further beyond the veil that
lies across the future than any of his day. He was, indeed, "ahead of his times"; he could foresee consequences where others were conscious only of the deeds
of the moment, the circumstances of the hour, caring
not at all how these might mold the future. Sometimes,
it is true, that vision of the future carried him ahead
too fast.

But it is not merely these traits that the son thinks
of with welling heart, nor of those qualities that the
fairies truly bestowed upon him. It was a precious herit-
age, indeed, to have a brave and handsome father,
noble always in his integrity and his ideals. It was a
great experience to behold how profoundly his earnest-
ness and sincerity influenced those with whom he came
into contact; how naturally they turned to him to lead;
how quickly his mind found new paths and how it was
never closed to new ideas; how persistently he espied
new deeds that needed to be done.

Yet this father means more than that. To his children he gave the picture of a world akin; no part of it
but had deep interest for him. Citizen of two lands, no
narrow nationalism could be his. He abhorred those
who seek by metes and bounds to stake out for their
selfish selves a part of the world to have it all their

own, letting the devil take care of the rest. He felt the world should be as free as the air; that no barrier of tariff or of trade or of law should hamper free movement of men and of goods. He hated no man for his color, and feared none because his was a different hue, a different tongue, another faith, a strange and baffling mode of life. Four years of battle and of carnage had made of him an uncompromising foe of war. He, long a leader in large affairs, friend of all the statesmen of his time, who had given his life to practical constructive effort, revolted with his whole soul from that sum of all villainies, war, which turns men into beasts, which destroys and never builds up, and never leaves the world but worse. Is it any wonder that he who writes this should share these views?

The years have passed, each more quickly than the last. Nothing dims the memory and the inspiration of that noble presence, of that unfettered soul that never harbored a sham, nor failed in fidelity to its ideals. But should these memories fade one by one, at the very last will be the recollection of an unfailing love, of generous and tender devotion. To all "his bounty was boundless as the sea." Immortality? There it lies! From heart to heart it leaps to warm, sustain, and spur, until the hour comes when, deathless, it wings its way to another resting place in the soul of a child.

To

AARON WISE

by

STEPHEN S. WISE

Free Synagogue, New York City

"A deep and withering sense of inferiority would have overcome me, had it not been for my Father's understanding, compassion, and, in the end, love."

*   *   *   *

"My Father gave me rebirth through the warmth and tenderness of his trust."

STEPHEN S. WISE

It is not easy to write of "What I Owe My Father," for one who is the equal, that is, the limitless debtor, of both Mother and Father. But, in one sense, I am surely nearer to my Father for I made his calling my own and my choice was supported and rejoiced over by him. I have often wondered in recent years whether like my Father I chose the ministry or whether I chose my Father's calling.

The affinity between my Father and myself, native or elective, was perceived by me very early in life, long before it would have been possible for me to have pondered upon or used these terms. I had a very early sense of certain things in my Father's life and in my own relation to them which are revived as I go back to them after the passing of fifty years.

At the risk of sounding priggish, I felt moved from earliest boyhood to take a protective attitude toward my Father. Even before I had become conscious of personal limitations and failures, I felt something akin to resentment against the world in relation to my Father. He was born to poverty that perhaps may fairly be described as decent, the poverty of the home of a Central European rabbi in the mid-nineteenth century. His Father was a bigoted saint, his mother an understanding saint, and his boyhood was touched by the exacting saintliness of a deeply devout and vastly learned rabbi

161

of a century ago. Hearing the tales of occasional though not uniform opulence in my Mother's childhood home led me to unreasoning resentment against the hardships my Father endured—without, it is true, a syllable of complaint by him in retrospect—throughout his childhood days. The difference between the comfort and security of my Mother's early home and the scantiness and the insecurity of my Father's home led me, I recall, to wonder why my Mother's people did not provide for my Father, in his hard, stern childhood—though, of course, they could not have done so for they did not know him.

Something else came to pass between us which meant that either we were born close to each other or else that we speedily entered into a relation than which nothing more beautiful and tender ever blessed the life of a child. Whatever may be held with respect to the validity of the postulates of modern psychology, I know that I was a younger brother, and that to a most gifted and attractive being, who inevitably, though always compassionately, outshone me in every way. At school he was brilliant despite his effortlessness, while I plodded on, as best I could, with distinctly mediocre talents withal never-ending effort. He won all hearts, and our Mother, as often happens, diverted to him not a little of the adoration of her Father whom my elder brother was fancied to resemble. A deep and withering sense of inferiority would have overcome me—and in truth it came very near to blighting my life—had it not been for my Father's understanding, compassion, and, in the

end, love. Out of his great heart overflowing with compassion came to me what I believe was at first little
more than pity for my plight, the pity of a robust and
in every sense sturdily loving Father for a son who
must have appealed to him as an "under-dog," in—
what was not yet styled—a psychic fray. No child
could have needed heartening more than I did, mark-
edly inferior as I was in gifts to an elder brother upon
whom all family attention was fixed and touching whom
alone there were radiant forecasts.

My Father gave me rebirth through the warmth and
tenderness of his trust. It was the generosity of his
understanding as man and the tenderness of his sympathy as parent that enabled him to discern my prob-
lem decades before I recognized it. It was not partiality,
for he, too, was enthralled to the elder brother and to
a younger sister and brother, but understanding of my
need, which understanding derived from out of the
magic of parental love. It was not as clear and simple
in his sight nor yet in mine as I, after a life-time, have
come to understand it to have been. But I have no
doubt—and once, before his early passing at fifty-two,
he hinted, with obvious reluctance after undue pressure
on my part, at this—that he sensed and pondered over
my need of something to help me overcome a feeling
of inferiority which, if left unchecked, was bound to
have a disabling effect upon my personality. Out of the
deeps of his understanding and love he gave me the
beginning of self-trust. Better than that, he imbued me
with the resolution not to accept handicaps as disable-

ment, to refuse to regard difficulty and defeat as inter-changeable. And all this he did with unbelievable ten-derness, and, to be truly just to his finely rounded per-sonality, with that unfailing humor which saved the situation from what might easily have deteriorated into sickly sentimentality. Is it less than rebirth to be given, after an agonizing period of youthful self-distrust, the beginnings of faith in one's self?

But there was, there is, much more that I owe my Father. Oft-times in the course of the years, I have been moved to feel that my words were little more than the formulation of his thoughts and that my acts were in a very real sense the embodiment of his aims, my deeds the fulfillment of his dreams. Thus he was a resolute and uncompromising idealist equal to every de-mand of his fine and genuine idealism despite obstacles and barriers.

The major handicap was bound up with the circum-stance that he came to these shores at the age of thirty, a master of the German tongue, and, as he imagined, too late to overcome the difficulties of English speech. And this at a time when the passion for assimilation among the German-born Jews in America was so in-tense that the one insufferable disqualification of the rabbi was an imperfect command of the intricacies of English grammar and the niceties of English enuncia-tion, though usually most of the flock were far more innocent of English—though they did not know it—than the shepherd. I remember the utter courage with which, from time to time, he expressed in his pulpit his

convictions on controversial issues—social, industrial,
ethical. Then arose misunderstanding on the part of the
simple, kindly folk to whom he ministered. The misunderstanding was due either to careless reporting or to
malevolent tale-bearing on the part of a "brotherly
colleague."

Long, long ago, it must be quite forty-five years, I
heard him lament *"de Sklaverei der Kanzel,"* the en-
slavement of the pulpit. Insofar as I founded the pulpit
of my Synagogue upon the rock of pulpit freedom, insofar as I have done what one man could do to liberate
the pulpit of church and synagogue, to free it for the
unreserved and unchallengeable utterance of truth, I
have but finished what he began, and won what he inevitably failed of. Paraphrasing Whittier for yet another moment, to "right the wrong" is comparatively
easy after the wrong has been clearly descried and
bravely resisted by another. To "sing the song" is a
minor task by the side of holding to the changeless
faith that "something alway alway sings."

One of the major interests of my life I owe chiefly to
my Father—that is, Zionism. It may have been in my
blood, but it was the tide of his devotion which bore it
to the heart of my being. Without being, as his Father
was, Orthodox, his ardent adherence to Zionism is one
of the earliest and sweetest memories of my life. Our
first lesson in saving and giving we got as very young
children in our home, in connection with humble am-
bassadors from the Land of Israel, into whose little
tin cups we placed our scant savings, that these might

in turn be given to satisfy needs in the Holy Land. The pilgrimage of his Mother to Palestine at seventy, after her husband's death, made the land my Father's second home. Alas, he was not fated to fulfil the wish of his heart and journey thither. When the call of Theodor Herzl was sounded, I felt the summons to serve the cause of Zionism as if it were my Father's voice. And I have had ineffable joy throughout a generation in a service which was blended of the longing to help, however humbly, to reestablish the Jewish National Home in Palestine, and to do the work he would have loved and thirsted to do, had he not passed on the very eve of the Herzl epoch.

Throughout my ministry mine has been—it might be called—the mystic sense of finishing my Father's uncompleted tasks, of rejoicing in opportunities denied him to utter the word and to undertake the task that ought to have been his own. His clear understanding must have made him very doubtful with respect to the adequacy of my qualifications for the ministry. I have not his learning, his power over men, his gifts of imagination and of persuasiveness. He could not wholly have believed in my power to carry on, but he moved me to believe that I must go on and do what it lay in me to do for the sake of the cause and, what was almost equally precious to me, for his sake.

To

JOSEPH J. WOOLLEY

by

MARY E. WOOLLEY

Mount Holyoke College

I remember as if it were yesterday the criticism of a parishioner . . . who, when asked why she looked askance at the new minister, replied that she could not trust any minister who went up stairs three steps at a time. . . .

* * * *

United with his energy, his fearlessness, and his determination, was a group of qualities quite different. If limited to a single adjective, I think I would choose the word "human."

MARY E. WOOLLEY

ONE of my father's outstanding characteristics was boundless energy. I remember as if it were yesterday, the criticism of a parishioner soon after he went to Pawtucket, Rhode Island, who, when asked why she looked askance at the new minister, replied that she could not trust any minister who went up stairs three steps at a time. The ability to perform that particular feat—much admired by his children, may I add, if not by all of his parishioners—disappeared in course of time but the *energy* remained. Even within a few weeks of his death, he rode, a favorite exercise, a horse that was not a "mollycoddle," for there are such even in the equine world. To this endowment of energy which he conserved by a sane and wholesome life, must be attributed in large measure his capacity for hard work. The amount which he accomplished was more remarkable because it was sustained month after month, year after year, not done by spurts.

Together with this energy went absolute fearlessness. My mother often said with a note of half-envious admiration, "I think your father does not know what it is to be afraid of anything"—and I imagine she was right. A few years ago I attended a reunion of the Eighth Connecticut Volunteers, the Regiment of which my father was chaplain during the Civil War, and among the stories which the little group of veterans told me

169

was one of an incident before Fredericksburg. A soldier
had come with a message to my father's tent and, when
the shells began to fall alarmingly near, mounted his
horse for a hasty retreat. My father's only comment
was, "Let 'em shoot. I'm going to finish my breakfast."

Among my earliest recollections is the thrill of terror
not unmixed with delight, with which I saw the horse
my father was riding on Memorial Day, dance with the
band, only his hind feet on terra firma, his front ones
pawing the air. In later days, one of his keen pleasures
in his hardly won leisure moments was to "break" colts
for a friend, and I have seen him drive through Pawtucket streets at a pace which I am sure would also
have "broken" the speed laws, if there had been any in
those days.

That absolute fearlessness was shown in his work.
Many a time, at midnight or later, the doorbell would
ring and an entire stranger appear, to summon my
father to some case of critical illness in an unknown
or undesirable part of the city, a summons which he
never for an instant hesitated about answering. His
courage was of the militant order—a courage which he
kept to the end. Through the last painful hours of his
life, he showed only fortitude and calmness, occasionally repeating some favorite passage, the 23rd Psalm
or "Crossing the Bar," a poem which he dearly loved.

This courage was moral as well as physical; he never
flinched from doing the thing which he thought he
ought to do. And if he realized that he had made a mistake in judgment, as he sometimes did, for he was nat-

urally impulsive, he was not afraid to admit it and to change his course.

My father was a man of iron determination. I never knew him to give up a thing because it was difficult— on the contrary difficulties seemed but a stimulus to greater effort. "One should never give up a plan because of bad weather" was his theory and practice, a theory and practice which he applied far more widely than to climatic conditions.

His was not a life of ease; all through his years from boyhood on, he battled with difficulties and "the will to achieve" became a habit of his life. It was not a selfish habit, far from it. He used it for others, for causes and for individuals.

In thinking about my father during these years since he left us, I have felt that his power came from a union, what might be called a "blend" of qualities, not always found in one individual. United with his energy, his fearlessness, and his determination, was a group of qualities quite different. If limited to a single adjective, I think I would choose the word "human." He was the friend of more people, of all sorts and conditions, than any one I have ever known. Some people make a pose of democracy, some make a deliberate and honest effort to be democratic. It was no effort on my father's part. He liked human beings, liked to be with them, met them on the plane of their interests, was one of them. He wanted to do them good but it was not at all in a Pharisaical sense. It was rather that he saw the possibilities of good in human nature and wanted to "set it free."

This friendliness was not undiscriminating; he had a keen insight into human nature, would occasionally "touch off" a character in an unforgettable way, never with malice. For a man who was impulsive, occasionally impatient at shortcomings, he was wonderfully charitable except to hypocrisy or meanness. Nor did he admire a type which he characterized by a criticism no harsher than "Isn't he a *softly* man?"—an adjective which I have failed to find in the Dictionary, but which had a perfectly definite meaning for him!

I do not need to tell those who were his boys and girls, what a tender spot he had in his heart for young people. He was interested in their work, their education, their church life, their amusements. Dr. Meiklejohn has referred more than once to the fact that when he was a boy my father was one of the most interested of "fans" at the ball games.

It was not only the local ball games that held a lure for him. If late at the evening meal during the season of the "League" games, it did not take shrewdness to guess where he was! An afternoon at a ball game or a tennis tournament, an evening of checkers or backgammon with an opponent that would put him on his mettle—he would enter into these with the zest and enthusiasm of a boy. David Starr Jordan, when President of Stanford University, gave an inspiring address to students on "Life's Enthusiasms" based on the cynical remark in a French novel, "My son, we should lay up a stock of absurd enthusiasms in our youth or else we shall reach the end of our journey with an empty heart, for we lose a great many of them by the way." My father certainly kept life's enthusiasms. He brought back from his European and Near East trips, glowing and vivid accounts which some far more traveled travelers do not equal; he gained from reading and observations more accurate and enthusiastic knowledge of certain subjects than is sometimes acquired in the classroom. He was particularly fond of astronomy, always reading the articles which Professor Upton, of Brown University, published for a series of years in the Providence *Journal,* keeping track of astronomical discoveries and frequently calling the attention of some less observant member of his family to the beauty of the skies or to the position and brilliance of a planet.

His enthusiasm for individuals was almost boyish. He was a hero-worshipper. The heroes of the ancient world; the heroes of the Civil War, first and foremost Abraham Lincoln, to whom he gave veneration long before it became fashionable; Grant and Burnside and Lee and Stonewall Jackson, for the mere fact that the last two were "on the other side" made no difference with his enthusiasm for the men themselves; the men of his own day, who achieved something fine—all were enrolled in his hall of fame and given unstinted admiration.

The tender human side of his nature was never more evident than in his love for animals. His love for horses was known wherever he was known. It was not only

that he liked a good horse who could "go well,"—they
were his friends, to whom he gave personal affection.
A close second to horses, came dogs and birds. Little
"Sergeant Rags" who accompanied him from the Spanish War, and many another dog, of earlier days, were
as devoted to their master as he was to them. Perhaps
his greatest personal extravagance was in the line of
birds. The trained canaries, Japanese robins, bullfinches
that we had in the course of years, would have stocked
an aviary! A harmless and an appealing extravagance.
A mind-picture of my father that I love to recall, is of
him in front of a cage, whistling, for the bird to answer,
or holding it on his finger.

A keen sense of humor often relieved a situation or
helped to lighten a burden, sometimes a *saving* sense.
My brother recently reminded me of the visiting clergyman who preached on and on, until the hour glass, if we
had had one, would have been well along its second
round, when my father leaned forward and pulled his
coat tail! I think his love of a good story came only
second to his love of a good horse, and was a source of
pleasure to us all. As children, we listened spell-bound
to the rapid-fire of wit and anecdote at the Monday
luncheons which he and Doctor Behrends had together
at the latter's home or at ours, and when other guests
—especially those of the clerical persuasion—were at
our table. Often he would come home chuckling over
some witty remark that he had heard down town, as
for instance, a hack-driver's answer to his question,
"for whose funeral a long line of carriages was in at-

tendance," "It happens to be a wedding, Mr. Woolley, but I suppose it is all the same." One of his favorite bits of repartee was that of an old apple woman on the dock at Queenstown when he asked her why she was a fruit-seller, "For money, money, money. I want every kind of money and all the money I can get, except matrimony, and the Lord knows I've had enough of that."

My father was a liberal man, liberal in material things, giving out of proportion to his means, as we see it, perhaps not as God sees it. He was liberal in his attitude toward his fellow men. If there had been a difference, he was ready—and more than ready—to bury the hatchet. That characteristic is strikingly illustrated by an incident in the Spanish War which he loved to recall. At Camp Alger the First Rhode Island was stationed near a Tennessee Regiment of which the colonel had also served in the Civil War, but on the Confederate side. He and my father became great friends and one day, visiting a battlefield of the Sixties, the colonel throwing his arm affectionately over my father's shoulder, said, *"We* have been here before, haven't we, Chaplain?"

He had a keen sense of honor, particularly noticeable in his attitude toward the confidences of others. A sort of father confessor for many people, his own household knew singularly little about the personal affairs of the community. As for scandal, he would have none of it. One of the characteristics of which I am proud, was the cleanliness of his thought and speech, as well as of his act. He never rolled an unsavory morsel under his tongue.

Of my father's conception of his work there are two or three characteristics that seem to me outstanding. He had no patience with a religion that was not "backed" by the life. I remember a remark of many years ago, that some prayers went no higher than the ceiling and his amusement when a member of the church indignantly protested against this characterization of his devotion. "What made you think that I was referring to you?" was my father's only comment.

His belief in the social mission of the church was far in advance of his day. The conception of the church as an exclusive organization was abhorrent to him. He had no sympathy with the custom of selling pews, still less with the pew holder who was "disgruntled" if he found his seat taken by strangers. "The church" existed for the people; he would have it always open for them, the centre of their life. His ideal was that it should be a power for righteousness, in the community, with emphasis both on "righteousness" and on "power." Anything short of this ideal was a failure, no matter how prosperous it might be as an organization.

This "reminiscence" is of my father—but I cannot close without a word about my mother. A good friend of ours said of her the first time I saw him after she had left us, "This world seems a poorer place when so bright a spirit has gone out of it." She made our home a heaven on earth, "a place where strife was shut out— and love was shut in." But that does not mean that her love was a selfish one or that her influence was limited. That influence was far wider than she dreamed, even among people whose names she had never heard. A teacher passing our house daily on her way to school said to me, "I never met your mother, but I shall never forget her face at the window or the influence that it has had on my life." Often I have thought of a remark of hers in answer to a criticism of mine, which I think strikes the keynote of her character. I was young then and foolish and my mother's habit of nodding to her friends in the different parts of the auditorium before the service began, seemed to me not the "proper" thing! She listened patiently to my criticism and without questioning my judgment said very simply, "Then I'll just smile at them."

The secret of these lives, held in such dear remembrance, was their Christianity—a secret which we guessed even as children, and which has been an inspiration throughout the years.

SHORTER TRIBUTES

ARTHUR BRISBANE:

"Whatever I have, I owe to my father and mother. And I owe them good and useful work which, I am afraid, will never be done."

ARTHUR CAPPER:

"Three things my father impressed upon his children—honesty, industry, thrift. On my tenth birthday anniversary he gave me a copy of *Poor Richard's Almanac*. All the wonderful things that have come into our lives since, and all the wonderful theories that have been propounded, have not been able to shake the influence of father and his birthday present."

ROBERT A. MILLIKAN:

"A strong sense of duty and a fearlessness and rigid honesty in the following of convictions."

JOHN R. MOTT:

"Among the many contributions which my father has made to my life, in some respects the most highly multiplying was the inculcation, by example and precept, of the wise use of leisure."

ADOLPH S. OCHS:

"I cannot give myself the whole credit for what I have been able to do towards maintaining and promoting moral and ethical standards. I was born with them and raised by parents who inculcated them in me by precept and example, and appeal to reason. I was so completely under parental care, guidance and supervision that up to the time I was seventeen years old I handed my pay envelope to my father unopened, and received my small weekly allowance of spending money. My parents were God-fearing and pious. The Golden Rule was deeply engraven in their hearts. Religion, Literature, Music, Art and the finer things of life surrounded us, and were included in the family curriculum."

DANIEL A. POLING:

"His courage and his faith were and are outstanding. The former never wavered and the latter has always been on the march."

UPTON SINCLAIR:

"As I think it over, I am inclined to say that what I got from my father was idealism. Although he had to live among the Yankees, he thought of himself as an old-fashioned Southern gentleman, and he lived up to old-fashioned ideals of honor and courtesy. There was something very quixotic about it, but it had a fine flavor of sentiment which I think I imbibed through the skin, as it were."

NATHAN STRAUS:

"My father always said that if dishonesty was a virtue, it would be his policy to be honest. He told us this from personal experience. Both my father and brother Isidor had the same view, and I found that they were more than correct."

HENRY VAN DYKE:

"What do I owe to my father? Everything. He was my best friend: a parent who knew how to be patient with an unruly child; a preacher of joyful faith, who practiced what he taught; a good companion in the woods and the library; a fearless man with a kind heart; a Christian without pretense or bigotry; a true American gentleman of the democratic type. Every day I give thanks for him."

BURTON K. WHEELER:

"Devotion to his family.

Sincerity and unflinching loyalty to his ideals.

His belief in the great moral and religious principles of right living."

THE EDITOR CLOSES THE BOOK

THE story of the making of this book may be of interest. While on a railroad journey, a companion of the Editor related an incident in his boyhood in which his father played a prominent part, and added, "That left a lasting impression." Immediately, there was a response, "That makes a call for a new book—in which ten or twelve well-known people will be asked to give an informal story of what each owes to his father. They will be asked to portray traits in their fathers which they consider important in the making of their own lives—to the end that the youth of today may be benefited by ideals and principles that have proved powerful."

The Editor was fortunate in finding a publisher who from the beginning has taken a sympathetic interest in his work. Fortunate, too, in finding such eminent people willing to tell these intimate narratives, for the good of this generation.

It will have been borne in upon the reader, as he has gone from story to story, that nothing is more important than family life. He will have realized that the Family is more sacred than either State or Church.

The reader—be he parent, child, or teacher—will have seen, through these pages, some important things to avoid, and some to cultivate. While former methods may not be imitated, certainly the principles and ideals that governed in the homes here described will bear close study. These stories have revealed some of the principles that are essential to any enduring civilization.

S. S.